D1527191

Experiencing Spiritual Encouragement

Devotional Thoughts from the Word

Ann Varnum

Experiencing Spiritual Encouragement

Library of Congress Control Number: 2011924738

ISBN 9780983244103

"I've followed Ann Varnum's devotionals for several years and I *love* every single one I've ever heard or read. I feel God's Spirit through her words, and they bless me. I am convinced her insights and wisdom are a direct result of a close walk with the Lord."

Jeannie St. John Taylor
Author, Illustrator, Speaker, Columnist

"Week after week, Ann challenges and encourages me through her devotionals. She never fails to 'hit the nail on the head' with personal illustrations and timely Scripture. If you desire to be lifted up with the truth, you will love her book!"

Kathy Gannon
Homemaker

"As I find it difficult to compress my praise for Ann Varnum and her work into a single comment, I invite everyone to read Experiencing Spiritual Encouragement. Not only will you be blessed by these devotionals, you will discover the heart of a wonderfully inspired and gifted writer."

Mike Coe
Author

"Her words 'hit home' regardless of one's own personal beliefs. In my opinion, a compilation of her articles provide us with a wonderful source for continuing daily inspiration and encouragement."

Larry Hicks
Retired high school principal

For a number of years I have written devotionals that have been published in the "Dothan Eagle" here in Dothan, Alabama. The letters, e-mails, phone calls and even personal comments have been overwhelming. To all of you who have inspired me to put all of these articles in a book, this one is for you. I hope it brings great comfort and encouragement to my readers as the writing has been to me. God Bless.

Acknowledgments

I would like to thank my publisher and friend, Martin Murphy, who is the primary person responsible for this book. Special thanks to my nephew Jack Lavallet and his co-worker, Robert Gunner, for taking my idea and creating the perfect cover for the book; Linnea McClellan, who initially invited me to write for the EAGLE; Peggy Ussery who allows me to invade her space in the paper and to the DOTHAN EAGLE for publishing my devotionals each month.

Foreword

It has always been my desire to encourage the readers of the devotional thoughts that I write and I am deeply humbled by the wonderful response I have been getting from those who read my columns. My prayer is that in this collection of my devotionals there will be a word of encouragement for each reader. Above all, I want to bring Glory to our Wonderful Lord, Jesus Christ, who knows everything about us and loves us anyway. I now invite you to experience with me spiritual encouragement.

Table of Contents

I am the Lord of all your Nesting Places

Sitting on my back porch that fall morning in 1990, I was totally exasperated, to say the least. When my husband's business had suddenly taken a turn for the worst, he had put our house up for a much needed loan, and now, since we couldn't pay it back, the bank was going to foreclose. "Why, Lord?" I angrily cried out. "I can't believe you won't do something to save our house!" His reply was the last thing I wanted to hear.

Our ordeal actually began when my husband returned from a men's spiritual life retreat. A friend of ours, Al Whittinghill, had spoken on the biblical account of Abraham and Lot. He had emphasized the scriptural admonition not to be unequally yoked. That week-end, Jerome came home with the conviction that he had to somehow separate himself from his partner, who was not a Christian. When he told me, I immediately agreed with him. After all, I had watched my husband become more and more agitated every day. He needed relief, and so did I! My vision, at the time, was that his partner would leave and allow us to keep the business. As it turned out, however, the partner insisted that he wanted the business, and we walked away with only a small salary for one year.

We were obedient to separate ourselves from a partnership that was really not of God. Since we also owned a small garden center, we assumed that God would just naturally bless our gardening operation. This was not the case! First, there was the freeze that killed most of our plants (even those under cover). It was the coldest December on record. Next, when Jerome drove up north to get more trees, his van broke down on a deserted highway. He knew if he couldn't get it started, not only would the plants freeze, but he probably would as well. What to do? This was before the wide use of cell phones and who would he call anyway? Jerome stepped out into the deserted highway but no vehicles were in sight. He waited......at last, a car approached. In desperation he prayed while waving his hands, but the driver refused to even slow down. Minutes passed that seemed more like hours, and it was getting darker and colder by the second.

Finally, another car was spotted in the distant horizon coming his way. Frantically, my husband began waving toward the driver, but it, too, passed him by. Just then, with a stroke of God's guidance, Jerome spoke aloud into the stark darkness, "Stop in the name of Jesus!" By then, the car was already way past where he stood, but suddenly, it stopped. The driver began backing the car up to where my freezing husband was standing.

The rescuer was an elderly black minister. He later told Jerome he rarely travelled that way at night and knew better than to pick up strangers by the side of the road in that isolated stretch of road. "However," he smiled as he told Jerome, "I believe the Good Lord just told me to stop just then, so I obeyed." After hearing my husband's side of the story, they both rode together into the next little town having a wonderful time in the Lord.

Again, God had shown up just in the nick of time. The next morning, repairs were done on the van, and Jerome was able to return to our home in Dothan. The plants, however, did not fare so well.

Instead of seeing God's hand in blessing our business, the reverse seemed to be true. No matter how hard Jerome worked, nothing seemed to pan out. The killing blow came when our leased land was sold out from under us. Even though we challenged it in court, we lost.

The next few weeks were very difficult ones. I had developed some kind of strange virus that mimicked lupus symptoms. I had previously been diagnosed with this disease in 1971 and after almost dying, it had apparently gone into remission. Now, I feared, I would be critically ill again. My poor husband had to not only make provisions to move our garden center to a new location, but he also had to look after me. Those were very difficult days, and we were really strapped financially.

Through a series of events, Jerome and I were able to secure a small business loan, and we re-opened a manufacturing site like his original one. By then, his ex-partner had gone out of business, so there was no non-compete issue involved.

At last, we breathed a sigh of relief, "God is finally going to bless our business because we have been obedient to do what He required!" We believed. But, God's timing is not like ours. He waits until the very best time to fulfill His promises to us. The wait, however, seemed forever to us!

One day, Jerome came home to tell me one of his employees foolishly, and against direct orders, had willfully climbed out on a cloth awning and had fallen through- breaking his leg. We believe now that it was a deliberate act so he could sue us, and sue us he did! His wife also sued us for a huge sum for "loss of marital relations for a time" (Due to the broken leg!) The man was in his late 50's and since no one else would hire him, Jerome, out of compassion, had done so. Now, this was the way he was paying us back. In spite of vast numbers praying for us, we lost in court and a judgment was issued against us for $325,000 plus $50,000 for the man's wife; a total of $375,000.

After that, the handwriting was on the wall. We had to declare bankruptcy and walk away with practically nothing again. That's when the Lord spoke to me that fateful morning when I was crying over the loss of my home. I'll never forget it. "I am the Lord of all your nesting places." My response was not very spiritual, I'm afraid. "God, I don't want to hear one thing about birds and nests. I just want to keep my home! If I were God, I wouldn't treat my children like this!" To that, He didn't respond.

As Paul Harvey always says.... "And now, for the rest of the story." As I look back, I can hardly believe all the events that have led up to the present time. It was just as if God had put together an intricately detailed travel plan much like one would set up a box of dominoes until one "happening" would trigger the setting off of the entire chain leading up to God's highest and best plan for our lives. Through all our disappointments, trials and loss, God was behind the scenes waiting to grant us the true desires of our heart.

In late 1990, we were able to get a townhouse after moving out of our home. Jerome had managed to sell his business to a group of powerful business men because they were interested in a new product he was helping to develop. Later, however, because he refused to betray the original designer's secrets of the patented product, the new owners dismissed him, and suddenly he was unemployed again.

Holy Scripture points out hope in the middle of a tough time. "But blessed are those who trust in the LORD and have made the LORD their hope and confidence. They are like trees planted along a riverbank, with roots that reach deep into the water. Such trees are not bothered by the heat or worried by long months of drought. Their leaves stay green, and they go right on producing delicious fruit" (Jeremiah 17:7-8, NLT). We knew that no matter what happened to us – with or without a job or even a home, God loved us and He would always take care of us.

It was about this time that our journey took an amazing turn. My sister, Martha, and her husband, Jack, decided to invest in helping us start a new business. Jack's expertise as an executive with Kimberly Clarke Corporation was a real plus, and ultimately, we purchased a huge 64 acre farm together and a plot of ground near the highway in front of the farmland for the business.

Our new "nesting place" sits on an eight acre pond about three quarters of a mile down a winding dirt road just behind the business. It is a lovely A framed dwelling with rustic wood and glass windows covering the wrap around porch. We have a beautiful open den, kitchen, dining area, four bedrooms and two and a half bathrooms.

It's my dream home! We have 3 dogs, a cat, geese, ducks and even "pet" catfish that come to our dock for feeding every day. Our children (and now grandchildren) love where we live. Our home has been the center for numerous Bible studies, family gatherings and visiting guests. We do the grandchildren's big birthday parties here, and rest, always in the faithfulness of Our God who is always "The Lord of all our nesting places".

And, we are here until He moves our nest.

A Christmas Reprise

Before we launch too far into a new year, I am reminded that the year ahead of you is going to be just what you make it to be. That is, if you believe that God loves you and that no matter what you see, He is in control. A true believer is reminded that our position in Christ causes us to be "giving thanks always for all things to God the Father in the name of our Lord Jesus Christ" (Ephesians 5:20). Granted, that is often a hard one to follow especially if we just lost a job, experienced the death of a loved one or perhaps faced some other traumatic circumstance in our lives. However, God would not have given us the command to do this, if He didn't require us to do it. With each directive our Father gives His children, He always includes the ability for us to accomplish it.

To illustrate this, I would like to share a story told by Drue Duke from Sheffield, Alabama. It seems that Drue had stood in line with her little boy for over 30 minutes waiting to speak to Santa Claus. As each child got his turn, they each requested a whole pile of toys. One by one, the list grew longer and longer. Finally, there was only one little boy ahead of her son and she hoped that child would not also have an endless list to request. As the little fella crawled into Santa's lap, he just settled into a corner of his arms and snuggled down. "What do you want me to bring you, young man?" Santa asked. "Anything you want to" the child replied. "You always know just what to bring me." This seemed to take Santa by surprise, but finally he asked, "Well, is there anything you want to tell Santa?" The little boy nodded and said "I love you." And with that, he stretched his neck and kissed Santa's face above the false whiskers. Then he was ready to climb down and went skipping off down the mall leaving the old man portraying Santa trying to hold back the tears that were slipping down his cheeks."

Drue went on to say that the lesson the little boy taught her will always be remembered. That night as she knelt to pray, she confided that she made no requests of God but just confessed to him that He always provided her with everything she needed and that she just wanted to say, "I love you."

This just may be one of the soundest theological topics you will ever read. Even though we are invited to "ask for what we need" and then to be thankful for what He chooses to bring us, evidently this little boy had the right concept even though he was just talking to Santa. He already trusted him to bring what he needed because that's what he always did. Is your New Year's prayer list like this? My prayer for next year is that God will create within us a grateful heart and a loving spirit.

Can you Ever go Home Again?

With the advent of "recycling" being such a prominent part of our present culture, it is not surprising that families are experiencing this very similar phenomenon as more and more children are returning home to live again with their parents.

The reason for these offspring coming back home is usually after they have failed in some area of their lives. It could be the result of dropping out of college, going through a divorce or facing a financial crisis. Whatever the excuse, multitudes of young adults are pouring back into their parents' homes.

From personal experience, years ago, I had to return to my family home due to a very serious illness. My Dad and Mom were so protective of me that I felt like I was 16 again and an invalid. They meant well, but it was a very difficult time for us all.

Much later, I was on the receiving end of returning children. Each of our three kids for one reason or other came back to live in our home. All I can say is my husband and I learned an awful lot during those times.

One thing we realized was that we couldn't treat them exactly like we did when they were growing up. These children were technically adults who had lived on their own for a period of time. Yet, they had come back to what they had believed was a "safe haven" in their time of need.

At the same time, we had our home and our set of rules to live by. It is obvious that we made it through those times with our mutual love and respect for each other intact.

In counseling other parents who face the same dilemma of returning offspring, we explain their possible options. These parents can always refuse to let their children come home. They can allow them to return and continue to treat them like they did when these kids were growing up or they can work out a compromise. You still have to have parameters. Your child will respect you far more if you uphold your standards while still respecting their rights and their independence. It's a tough tightrope to walk but well worth it. One day they will leave again and you will miss them. Very rarely they will continue to stay with you. If that should happen then at some point in time you might consider asking them to move, but then, that's an entirely different situation.

Whatever decision you make about allowing your children to come home, just remember these very kids might one day be the parent of your future grandchildren. Whatever you do, don't jeopardize that potential relationship. It's too wonderful to mess up.

God's guidance is very critical at this time and His Word is your best option.

- "If any lacks wisdom, he should ask God who gives generously to all without finding fault, and it will be given to him" (James 1:5, NIV).

- "Trust in the Lord and do good; dwell in the land and enjoy safe pasture. Delight yourself in the Lord and He will give you the desire of your heart" (Psalm 37:3, NIV).

Do you desire the right relationship with your children or with your parents? The time may come when a child has to go home again or, as a parent, you wind up having returning children. With God's help, you can have a new and rewarding relationship for nothing is impossible with God.

Give Away the Corn in your Crib

Years ago a simple carpet cleaner from Texas named Milton Green came to Dothan and set our town on its ear. His understanding of the Bible was learned while he was facing a death sentence due to his failing heart. In his desperation and fear, Milt ultimately turned to the Lord and became a Christian. From that time on, he wanted to give away what he had learned during those troubled times. He called it "having corn in your crib." The meaning, of course, is to share the spiritual truths that one has stored in his heart especially when passing through testing or trials. What a believer has found to be true in his life's experiences will evidently be indelibly stamped on the heart.

The Bible instructs Christians in these terms: "Praise be to the God and Father of our Lord Jesus Christ, the Father of compassion and the God of all comfort, who comforts us in all our troubles, so that we can comfort those in any trouble with the comfort we ourselves have received from God" (2 Corinthians 1:3-4, NIV). In other words, we are urged to always be faithful to "give away the corn in our cribs" or spiritual truths that have brought us peace and comfort.

A few years ago, a champion corn grower from the midwest was asked how he always managed to win the trophy at the State Fair for growing the finest corn. "That's easy" he answered; "I always give my corn away!" Unbelievable, but true. When his neighbors asked him about his winning corn, he would share some of those ears with the men on the adjoining farms. When planting time came and then the harvest, every neighbor who had received some of that corn had grown corn to cross-pollinate with his own corn, thus, causing his stock to be greatly improved.

Another Scripture with a promise of God's blessings when we are willing to help others is to "Serve wholeheartedly, as if you were serving the Lord, not men, because you know that the Lord will reward everyone for whatever good he does..." (Ephesians 6:7, NIV). That seems so inevitable, yet so many people find it difficult to share with others what trials they have been through even if they are common trials that all humans might face in life. Sometimes, individuals have to deal with their pride over finding themselves in dark circumstances, especially if a sin is involved.

Ask yourself, "What have you learned about walking with God that will encourage or strengthen someone else? Have you ever been in desperate times only to find that someone else has been in the same situation before and they are willing to talk to you about how they made it through those trying events? Didn't it help you a great deal? If you do have something you can "give away" in the area of strengthening someone else who is in sorrow of some sort, you simply must be willing to share it. If you do, both of you will be greatly blessed. Try giving away your "corn."

Remembering my Father

My father would have been the solution to all juvenile delinquency in America if he had been able to be the father to every teenager. He walked a fine line between holding our utmost respect while also instilling the "fear" of God in each one of his daughters. (There are four of us Jones girls.) Looking back, I know why we almost always did what he said. Somehow, he had the uncanny knowledge of knowing where each of us were at all times. As I remember it our dad was always consistent in what he promised. If he issued an ultimatum, we'd better do it or we reaped the consequences of our disobedience.

There was also the security of knowing he was always there to protect us. As a small child, when I awoke after having a bad dream, it was so comforting to hear my father snoring just down the hall in his bedroom. Growing up, we always used Daddy as an excuse for anything we honestly didn't want to do. We'd say, "If I did that, (like go with a group to steal watermelons) Daddy would kill me!" Our friends knew he would always find out and no doubt would administer the proper punishment.

He also didn't care if "everyone else was doing it" or it didn't matter if, "Dad, this is the style now." If it wasn't something he agreed to, then we didn't get to do it. Once, I put peroxide on my 'spit curls' and part of my bangs. Right after I had 'done the deed' it was time to eat dinner so I joined my family at the table. My hair was still wet when suddenly, as if he already knew what I had done, Daddy looked straight at me and said, "I saw____ (a friend of mine) today and she looks like a 'floozy' with that yellow stuff in her hair. Don't you ever let me hear that you'd do something like that or you'll be sorry.

After that, I made some excuse, went directly to the bathroom and washed the peroxide out of my hair. Thankfully, I had not had time to expose it to the sun so it would bleach out. I escaped the penalty for my misdeeds that time.

I remember the confidence I had when I reached into the glove compartment of my father's car at the gas station and could pull out a package of designated receipt books and simply write a big 'J' on the bottom where the blank was placed for the signature, and then I would hand it to the service station attendant. It never one time failed to work. I always pulled off with a tank full of gas.

Our father was the one who stayed up to make sure we got in on time. It also never bothered him to go to the door in his underwear to let us in. That's why our dates left quickly when the door started opening. Dad had a reputation for looking after his girls and it's a wonder any of us ever got asked out on a date.

One night Daddy watched me ride off with a group of students after church. Since we were so crowded, I had to sit in one of the boy's lap. That was before seat belts. When I got home that night, Daddy asked me to come sit on the side of his bed to talk to him. He was as gentle as he could be as he explained why it was not a good choice to sit in a boy's lap no matter how innocent it was. He didn't fuss, but we just talked. How I value those times with Daddy.

There's absolutely no way I could list all the wonderful time shared with our daddy. He was a strict but loving father. I truly believe that's where I first learned about God. I know now that since my father was a human being and, therefore, imperfect, he made his share of mistakes. God, on the other hand, is perfect and never makes a wrong move.

God's discipline is always for our own good and His Glory. He is forever our protector and never loses control. There were times my earthly father wasn't able to protect me even though he always wanted to. I had sometimes made bad choices and had to suffer the consequences. My father was always there to encourage and comfort me when I passed through some very dark times. My Heavenly Father was there as well. And, more importantly, God could take my messes and create a miracle out of them. That was something my caring biological father simply couldn't accomplish even though he would if he could have.

My father, J. P. Jones, grew up without his own father since he died when my daddy was only four. Since he had longed for an earthly daddy all his life, he made sure we didn't miss having one. He was "hands on" daddy in every sense of the word. He made sure he knew everything about his girls, just like God.

Psalm 121 describes how loving and protecting our eternal Heavenly Father is:

1. Lift up my eyes to the hill—where does my help come from?
2. My help comes from the LORD, the maker of heaven and earth.
3. He will not let your foot slip—he who watches over you will not slumber;
4. Indeed, he who watches over Israel will neither slumber nor sleep.
5. The LORD watches over you—the LORD is your shade at your right hand;
6. The sun will not harm you by day, nor the moon by night.
7. The LORD will keep you from all harm—he will watch over your life;
8. The LORD will watch over your coming and going both now and forevermore.

Looking back, I am so thankful I had the father that I had.

How to Turn Lemons into Lemonade

Jim Hall left me a book by Merlin Carothers entitled, "Power in Praise." As I read through it, I was reminded of his first book "Praise to Praise." Both books are based on two biblical directives. The first one is to "give thanks in all circumstances for this is God's will for you in Christ Jesus" (I Thessalonians 5:18, NIV). The second is similar to the first; "always giving thanks to God the Father for everything in the name of our Lord Jesus Christ" (Ephesians 5:20, NIV).

It is one thing to praise God in the midst of a bad situation. It is quite another thing to praise Him for everything that happens to us.

Years ago right after I had read Carothers first book, I got to put his instructions to work. Learning that I was having unexpected company for lunch, I rushed to whip up some quick sandwiches since I didn't have time to cook. The guest was an important one, and I wanted to impress him. Then, it happened. The jar of mayonnaise slipped from my fingers and crashed to the floor breaking into pieces.

How could anyone make a sandwich without mayonnaise? I wanted to scream as I looked down at the big mess of smashed mayonnaise. Then, I remembered. I was to always give thanks to God in every situation no matter what, so I hesitantly began to praise God that He was in control and that He loved me. Next, I remembered that I had to get the sandwiches ready, so I left the mess and rushed to prepare the meal. Soon, I was smiling as I started thanking God for the dropped mayonnaise. Suddenly, a strong urge led me to return to my pantry. As I pushed cans aside on the shelves, to my delight, there stood a new jar of Kraft Special Mayonnaise. I honestly didn't even remember when I had picked it up.

The end of the story reveals God's purpose. As I was obedient to praise God in that situation, my panic gave way to peace, and with a clear head, I proceeded with my task. By the way, our guest loved the sandwiches and he even insisted on cleaning up my mess, which he did quickly and completely.

Turning to God with thanksgiving and praise creates a change in the attitude of our hearts. It is evident it pleases our Father, too, as He delights in coming to our rescue when we are obedient to Him.

Just this weekend, my dear friend, Betty Jurashek came for a visit. She had just lost her husband Bob, and I wanted more than anything to comfort her. I had prepared a special breakfast casserole that I knew she would love. As we sat and chatted, I decided to pop the dish in the oven to cook it as least half-way so it wouldn't take long to finish it the next morning. Realizing my timer to the stove was broken, I set my microwave timer. Then, I returned to the den to continue my conversation with Betty. What I didn't realize was that my microwave timer did not signal like the stove timer. We were so busy talking that the casserole was forgotten and since the timer didn't "beep" I had no warning it was cooking way beyond the finished stage. About the time that Betty smelled it, but it was too late. The top was toasted thoroughly! Instead of getting all disturbed about it, we decided to laugh about it. When we peeled the top off, it was delicious. In fact, the crusty cheese topping was wonderful.

It reminded me of all the times I had burned the toast when my children were growing up. Since my toaster was broken and wouldn't pop up, in my early morning rush, I would often forget to manually pop the toast up. Obviously it would get way too dark. Since I didn't have time to cook more, I would simply scrape the burn off. If the children complained, I would remind them that they should be thankful that I was the only mother who took time to "decorate" their toast. Our oldest son Steve got so used to my "burned" toast that he started requesting overly dark toast when he went off to college.

Finally, do you know how Melba toast got started? You guessed it – from a mistake. Once, overly done toast was inadvertently served to a New York Socialite. When the waiter at the high-end restaurant discovered how dry the neatly sliced toast was, he immediately apologized and rushed to exchange it. The lady wouldn't have it – she actually loved it. And, that's how Melba toast was discovered. Obviously, too, it was named "Melba" after the delighted customer who loved it!

After all is said, we are all just taking a test. God is good all the time. He is not trying to harm us. He just wants us to trust Him no matter what we face in life. If we truly believe that, then we can always choose to take the "lemons" in life and turn them into something sweet and refreshing like lemonade.

Discovering Hope When it Seems Impossible

Today, we are facing a critical time in our country with the economic downturn just being the least of our problems. Our nation is in serious trouble with our morals and spiritual values being swept away by an onslaught of ungodly forces. What are we, as Christians, and our dear Jewish friends going to do about it? Sit still and whine? Or, rise up and do something? With the Judeo-Christian heritage that we have enjoyed from the formation of our country being under attack, we MUST rise up and fight. Our first and best plan of action is to fall on our knees and pray. Only our God can intervene at this time in our history and He is willing "If my people who are called by my Name will humble themselves and pray and seek my face and turn from their wicked ways, then will I hear from heaven and will forgive their sin and will heal their land" (2 Chronicles 7:14, NKJV).

In no way do I believe this Scripture refers to people who do not have a heart for God. Unbelievers have no power to do anything any different. God is calling HIS people to pray and come to repentance for most of all allowing this evil to happen to our country. Sometimes people think that going to church is no more than a social exercise and reading the Bible in order to find the true path to life has simply "gone out of style." Well, those misguided people are very wrong. God's Word as found in the Holy Bible is as alive and powerful as it has ever been. It can be trusted when nothing else works. God's promises are sure and no matter what anyone thinks, God is in control. "Our God

Reigns" is the name of a popular hymn and it is the absolute truth.

Maybe this week you got some bad news. You might have been a victim of downsizing or your salary has been cut radically. Who is going to take care of you and your family? Possibly you are facing a critical illness or your children are going through extreme difficulties. Who do you run to? The company you worked for has dropped you. Doctors say there is nothing they can do about your sickness and whatever can you do about your loved offspring? If any of the above fits what you are now experiencing, then look up! Pray this deeply spiritual prayer. It is one I pray all the time. "God, Help Me!" And, He will. If your motives are pure and you are His child, then you can always pray in faith, believing that He hears you. Just as in our personal needs, God is willing to move just as powerfully in our Nation's needs. Whether small or great, nothing can interfere with God's purposes and His plans. Remember, the Scripture points out hope in the middle of a tough time. "But blessed are those who trust in the LORD and have made the LORD their hope and confidence. They are like trees planted along a riverbank, with roots that reach deep into the water. Such trees are not bothered by the heat or worried by long months of drought. Their leaves stay green, and they go right on producing delicious fruit" (Jeremiah 17:7-8, NLT).

In closing, since Our Heavenly Father cares about everything which concerns us, I want to tell you about God's mercy in the case of a very sick cat that our son Steve had befriended. "Dusty" was a frail female cat who had a very painful abscessed tooth. It stuck out of her little mouth like a dagger and thus, she could not eat without pain. Steve had started feeding her canned food because she couldn't chew the dry food her neglectful owners were giving her. Steve was beside himself trying to do something for her but she wouldn't allow him to touch her mouth. His friend, a veterinarian, said that the bad tooth could make her very sick and possibly even kill her. When we arrived at his house for a visit, I knew that only God could "fix" her tooth. I prayed for a miracle and that the tooth would fall out on its own and that the infection would be healed. The very next morning, I heard our daughter-in-law on the front porch squealing with delight. "Come here!" she yelled. "Dusty's tooth has fallen out." We all ran to see, and there was Dusty purring and rolling around like a young kitten. The tooth was gone! If God cares that much about an ailing cat, how much MORE does He care about us, his children? Our place is to pray and believe.

·

God Cares About Everything that we Care About

She is just a dog. Not just any dog. She is my dog and I love her. I named her "Zelda" after the free-spirited wife of the famed writer F. Scott Fitzgerald. One day Zelda got hit by a car while she was running across the street. We didn't find her until about two days later, and I knew immediately that she was in bad shape. My husband crawled under the porch where she had somehow managed to drag herself and had to carefully pull her out. She had also suffered a great deal of scrapes and had a few gashes in her legs.

Grieving over "Zelda" I was faced with a decision as to what to do about her condition. After prayer, it came to me that Dr. Tim Tucker in Ozark was well-known for his orthopedic skills. He had also operated successfully on some pets belonging to friends of mine. So Jerome and I took our little dog to Ozark. After the x-rays, Dr. Tucker's partner didn't give us much hope. He even suggested we might need to carry her to a specialist in Auburn. However, I still believed that Dr. Tucker was the one who was to operate on "Zelda", and so I left her there.

The next day, I called to check on my dog and Dr. Tucker was already performing surgery on her. To my surprise, he answered the call himself. He explained how difficult it was. "I'm praying for you," I said, "and others are too." Very kindly he responded, "I know that you were supposed to call me right now. I just believe that the Good Lord will show me how to fix her."

Immediately after I hung up, I called some of my friends who also believe that God cares about our pets, and we prayed for God to work a miracle through Dr. Tucker. As we prayed, I was reminded of seeing a large painting of a surgeon who was operating with a super-imposed picture of Jesus surrounding him and guiding his hands. As I visualized that scene, I felt impressed to read from the Word of God. "For you, Lord, have made me glad through your work; I will triumph in the works of your hands" (Psalm 42:4, NIV). How perfect!

One hour later when I called Dr. Tucker again, he was so pleased to be able to tell me that God had indeed helped him do the complicated surgery. "It was extremely difficult to do, but somehow, it all worked. Zelda will be fine" he said. That was the miracle that I had been praying for.

For those of you who have pets, I hope it has encouraged you. For God created all creatures large and small. He does care about them all.

Lord, Please get this Burden off my Donkey

Do you ever wonder what really happened after the Good Samaritan rescued the man who had been beaten and robbed by thieves (Luke 10:27-37)? If anyone is familiar at all with the Bible, this is one incident that is often pointed to as an example of showing forth God's love to someone in need. Some prominent citizens and religious leaders had avoided coming near to where the wounded man lay, because they didn't want to be involved. However, the simple Samaritan made a conscious choice to help the poor man. The Samaritan went to the wounded man "and bandaged his wounds, pouring on oil and wine. Then he put the man on his own donkey, took him to an inn and took care of him" (Luke 10:34, NIV). When the Samaritan had to leave, he even made provisions with the innkeeper to continue helping the hurt stranger.

One can't help admiring this kindly fellow who did what was needed to help a total stranger. Now, what about you? Have you ever tried to help someone that you believed was genuinely in need? In most cases, when that occurs, you feel so good about doing that simple act of charity. Actually, that's why some people give to worthy organizations that help the poor and needy. God's children ought to have a desire to be a blessing to others. However, sometimes you catch yourself caught in a web of deceit similar to a spider's web. Let me explain.

Unfortunately there are certain individuals that spend their entire lives being "needy." Those are the people who always make it known that they don't have money to pay their light bill or car payment or whatever. Often, these are the same folks who never darken the door of a church. They spend their entire lives with a "victims' mentality." And, guess what? They can spot a Good Samaritan a mile away!

I always try to give money to help others anonymously. First of all, that way God receives all the Glory and not me. Secondly, when I know there is a genuine need, I still believe a person should pray about what he or she is to do about it. Is it important enough to call the church to help this person? Waiting on God's timing is of utmost importance, too. Have you ever owned a "yo-yo?" Remember how you could roll the toy away from you only to have it snappily come back? That's what happens sometimes when you "play the part" of a Good Samaritan.

Once my sisters and I were all together driving to Texas to take our sister Becki back home. Along the way, we stopped at a rest area. While we were there, two precious little blonde haired girls came up to us. One looked about nine and the other probably seven. They were telling my sister Becki that they were hungry and asked her to please give them some money. Being the sweet, tender-hearted person she is, Becki said, "Of course sweetheart." But, call it spiritual discernment or whatever, I interrupted and moved in to interview the girls myself. Mostly, children will eventually tell you the truth, so I asked, "Where do you two live?" One of the girls said cheerfully, "Oh, we live right over there on the other side of the highway." As I continued to talk to them, I discovered their parents were outside in a car, and that they came to the rest area every day to ask for money. Immediately, I promised them some food, and we all left the bathroom together. We decided to give them our packed sandwiches that were left from our own lunches. We went over to the car where the parents of the girls were sitting. "We want you to have this food so your children won't be hungry", I said. Never in my life before or since have I ever heard such vile language from both the father and the mother. Then, the man cranked up the car and sped off furiously.

Now, obviously, we could have given them some money, but these people were professional con artists, and they were training their children to be the same way. It really broke our hearts, so right then and there we prayed for that family and especially those girls.

Another story I recall is the time my husband tried to help a former drug addict. We gave him a job, found him a place to live and financed flying his estranged wife here to reconcile with him. We even took him to Reach-Out in Chattanooga, Tennessee, so he could be under the Biblical teaching of Kay Arthur. Whatever we did for him, however, it was never enough. He was constantly needing more and more. Then, one morning he didn't show up for work. We discovered he had loaded up everything we had given him or loaned to him and took off.

Even though this hurt us very much, we still believed we had offered him a chance to change. The choice was always his to make. I hope the wounded man in the story of the Good Samaritan appreciated what was done for him. Perhaps, the best way he could have expressed his thanks was to begin to reach out and help others.

The Word of God commands us to do the will of God, "not with eye service, as man-pleasers, but as servants of Christ, doing the will of God from the heart, with good will doing service, as to the Lord, and not to men, knowing that whatever good anyone does, he will receive the same from the Lord" (Ephesians 6:6, NIV).

God's Words of Encouragement Never Fail

No matter how long a person has been a Christian, there are times when the circumstances of our lives overwhelm us. Even if we know the Bible well and have always been faithful in our church, we are caught off guard when "bad news" comes. No matter what our need is, we can turn it over to our Father because we are never alone.

When we have a desperate problem, God in His Faithfulness always sends us a special message of hope. It may come while we are reading our Bible, or He may choose to send someone who has faced the same thing that we are experiencing. God does not waste our sorrows when we can share how in our time of need, God sent us His encouragement.

King David in the Bible would often "encourage himself in the Lord" when he faced impossible situations. Anyone can do this by simply bringing to remembrance all the times God provided for us when we were in a time of despair. Did God ever let you down? If you are His child, didn't He always make a way for you when there didn't seem to be a way?

God will often use another child of God to come along side of you. "Let us not give up meeting together, as some are in the habit of doing, but let us encourage one another" (Hebrews 10:25, NIV). More often than not, when tragedy strikes, a person is tempted to get alone and allow the sorrow to deeply fester in their heart. However, in times of trials, we need to drop all pride and call out to the body of Christ to come to our aid instead of staying home and grieving by ourselves.

Encouragement takes different forms. Today, our neighbor, Preston, called to say that he had been sad all day worrying about his sick father but after reading my last column, the good Lord used it to give him hope. Once when our money was really tight, Mrs. Nell Jones gave me $40. Even though I tried to give it back to her, she refused and told me that this was a gift from God. I figured if God could send me $40 out of the blue, then it was no big thing for Him to send the rest that we needed. He did.

Another time, we had a big payment due that was over $400. We had no idea how we would ever come up with that money, but Jerome and I prayed for God to provide. The very next day, we got a rebate check from our insurance that was totally unexpected. It was for the exact amount that we needed plus the price of a stamp to mail our bill. God always shows up just in time with what we really need, not what we may think we need. If He sent His beloved Son to die for us, how much more will He give us whatever else we need. Remember, we are all called to encourage each other. "So do not throw away your confidence, it will be richly rewarded. You need to persevere so that when you have done the will of God, you will receive what He has promised" (Hebrews 10:35-36.NIV).

God Instructs: "Open Your Mouth Wide"

A few weeks ago as I was on my way to work, the Scripture "Open your mouth wide and I will fill it" (Psalm 81:10, NIV) popped into my head. Immediately, I knew that this was the Scripture that I needed to close the testimony that I planned to share at a women's conference at Pine Level Baptist Church. I was going to open with one of my favorite biblical passages, "Ask, and it will be given to you; seek and you will find; knock and the door will be opened to you. For everyone who asks receives; he who seeks finds; and to him who knocks, the door will be opened" (Matthew 7:7-8, NIV).

For weeks, maybe months, I had been praying about what God wanted me to do for the rest of my life. As my husband and I have gotten older, I wondered how we would be able to survive physically and financially as we entered our latter years. In my youth, I always believed in asking God for what was needed and then trusting Him to supply. He has never once let me down. When I could not seem to discern which direction to go in, I continued to seek His Presence by sincere prayer. He always chose the right path for me, and I kept on "knocking" until I was sure my prayer was answered even if it didn't always happen on my timetable.

The instruction to "Open your mouth wide and I will fill it" is so powerful. It is found right in the middle of Psalm 81. The entire Psalm is all about how God with His love and power led His children (Israel) out of Egypt (bondage) and had always provided for them as they traveled across the wilderness. To make sure they continued to rely on Him, He instructed them to "open their mouth wide" just like little baby birds who fully expect their mother bird to provide them with the food they need. They open their mouths because it is in their DNA to expect to be fed. How much more trusting are these little creatures even when their physical eyes have not yet opened than we are, when we have physical eyes to see and spiritual eyes, as well, to discern.

My dear friend, Christian author and artist, Jeannie St. John Taylor, once told me about her desperate need for a pair of shoes. Her family, at the time, did not have extra money for a new pair of shoes but Jeannie knew that God had money for shoes, so she got down on her knees and prayed that God would send her just the right pair of shoes that she needed. Before she had finished her prayer, someone knocked on the front door. It was a lady who asked Jeannie's mother if it would be all right to give Jeannie a pair of shoes. Her mother, rather overwhelmed, said, "yes, of course!" It was not only a pair of shoes that fit Jeannie perfectly but it was a RED pair of shoes. It was just the color of the Sunday dress that her mother had just finished making for her. Imagine how that impacted the faith of that little girl!

When we commit to Him to obey by "opening our mouths wide," so He can fill them is just God's way of saying: "Trust in me expectantly and you just can't imagine how much I want to bless you and fill your life with good things."

Can Anyone Become a Saint?

"Blessed in the sight of the Lord is the death of His Saints" was the opening Scripture from Psalm 116:15 that Pastor Bob Baxter used to begin Mary Celeste Jones's funeral. The service gave tribute to the many years this Godly woman had faithfully served her Lord. From the time she received Jesus as her Savior as a young teen until her last breath on this earth at almost 97 years of age, Mrs. Mary had enriched the lives of her family and friends with her love of the gospel. The widow of a gentle country doctor, she brought up her two children to follow the Lord. When her older daughter, Camille, went off to college, Mrs. Jones moved to Dothan with her young son Carl, Jr.

Soon, Mary Celeste's faith began to increase as she experienced an even deeper intimacy with her Lord. Her former pastor Charles McGowan also spoke at her "Home going Celebration" commenting on how she used her home continually for Bible study and prayer meetings. She was a loving counselor to so many people. When friends visited in her home, they came away encouraged and blessed. She fixed many meals for all of us who loved her and always fed us spiritually as well. If ever there was a saint, she certainly was one!

"And, just what is a saint" you might ask. A pastor friend of mine explained to me that any true believer who had accepted Jesus by faith was just as much a saint as someone like Billy Graham. Even though that might be a little hard to believe, let me share the rest of this story. On the same day Mary Celeste Jones's funeral was held, that afternoon my husband and I attended a second funeral. Frank Stinson was buried in his Crimson Tide jacket wearing his matching Alabama tie and hat. Liked by everyone who knew him, Stinson was a jokester who enjoyed making people laugh. Often described as a "Character" or a "Sport" the former billiard champ was also a loving husband and father.

At his service, Stinson's son-in-law told a very touching story that Frank had shared with him years ago in confidence. When Stinson was a teen, he had attended a tent revival. During the meeting, he had felt drawn to the altar to find out about giving his heart to the Lord. His desire was squelched, however, because a skeptical evangelist grabbed "Stinky" (Frank's nickname) around the neck and ordered him to go back to his seat and quit fooling around and wasting the preacher's time. Frank Stinson never pursued a relationship with God after then until about ten months before he died while he was in the hospital recovering from a kidney problem, Frank was led to the Lord by a youth pastor. Always before that time, Stinson had been a good moral man but he certainly didn't qualify for "sainthood" until the day he repented of his sins and invited Jesus to save him. "Sainthood" then came naturally as a result of his having an exchanged life. At age 79, Frank Stinson died as just as much a saint as Mary Celeste Jones. They both entered Heaven together on the merit of Jesus Christ alone and not their own.

According to the words of Pastor Ron Mehl (who has also gone on to his eternal reward), "God can save anyone, change anyone, use anyone and bless anyone." Mehl pointed to the harlot Rahab who believed in God's power to deliver, so she hid the Hebrew spies and was rewarded for her deed by saving the lives of her entire household and was later listed in the lineage of our Lord Jesus.

Only God can change and strengthen a person and cause them to become "saints" worthy of His kingdom on earth to be used by Him and then later to inherit the gift of eternal life. In listing the heroes of faith, Hebrews 11:34b says of them " whose weakness was turned to strength" and in Ephesians 1:18 ,the apostle Paul writes: "I pray also that the eyes of your heart may be enlightened in order that you may know the hope to which he has called you, the riches of his glorious inheritance in the saints,...."

God is a Redeemer God

Some of my favorite life verses are found in the gospel of Matthew. "Ask, and it will be given to you; seek, and you will find; knock, and it will be opened to you. For everyone who asks receives, and he who seeks finds, and to him who knocks it will be opened" (Matthew 7:7-12). God will give good gifts and not evil to His children.

Another favorite verse of mine is found in the book of Psalms. It is found on a little plaque on my desk that reminds me of God's goodness. "Great peace have those who love Your law, and nothing causes them to stumble" (Psalm 119: 165).

God just loves redeeming His people, those things that are lost, those things that seem now impossible to be fulfilled especially prayers that seem to have gone unanswered to the point that you have all but given up all hope of ever seeing the answer. There are so many examples of God's intervention and redemption in the Bible. "Behold, I will save My people from the land of the east and from the land of the west: I will bring them back, And they shall dwell in the midst of Jerusalem. They shall be My people And I will be their God, In truth and righteousness" (Zechariah 8:7). AND THIS IS NOW ONE OF MY NEWEST PROMISES, because it is not just Israel God refers to, but also for those of us who are Believers today AND OUR OFFSPRING.

There have been times when we go through our most difficult situations that we feel that God is far away from us. Little do we know that in our darkness, He is usually working behind the scenes on our behalf.

In 1971, I spent the summer at Ochsner's Foundation Hospital suffering from lupus. I was told I would never be able to work again. But God: In 2011, I am still working and healthy.

In 1972, I went through a painful divorce that I did not want. I believed at the time that I would be alone for the rest of my life. But God: In May, 1973, I married my true soul mate, Jerome Varnum.

In July of 1974, I started work at WTVY in Dothan as the Hostess of A TV Talk Show.

When my husband sold his business and started to work for an exciting new company on the cutting edge of technology, I was thrilled that at last my prayers were answered. I had always believed that one day Jerome would get paid for what he knew and not for what he physically had to do. Then, the company closed and Jerome had a heart attack followed by open heart surgery. Because of this, he is unable to work. Soon, I will have to retire. What then? I know the answer to that. The same God who provided redemption for all those problems in the past, is the same God who will work in these difficult times as well.

Some of God's miracles along the way: My husband helped lead my ex-husband to the Lord. Every Sunday, we all sit together in church with our grandchildren.

Our oldest son's wife Nina, an attorney, is about to have our granddaughter any minute now at age 47 after we had given up all hope of them having a baby.

Even though many of our family members are not now walking with the Lord, I have the promise that one day they all will. God is forever faithful to His word. He will also supply every need we have whether we can sell our boat or the building where we had our business or not. God always knows best and

He is so creative, that He can do it His way, and in His timing. I am convinced of this because of who we are celebrating this time of year. It is the birth of the Lord Jesus Christ. There is no reason to fear for the Word of God says, "Do not be afraid, I bring you good news of great joy that will be for all the people. Today in the town of David a Savior has been born to you, he is Christ the Lord" (Luke 2:9).

HAS THIS SAVIOR BEEN BORN TO YOU? IF NOT, NOW IS THE TIME....

Can you Thank God for the Things You've Missed?

Teri and Jack can! When trying to adopt a beautiful little Chinese girl, they were rejected because it had been discovered that she had a twin. Through numerous pictures of the little child, they had become so attached to her and even chose the name "Jillian" for her. After the discovery that there were two babies, the name "Jacqueline" seemed to fit the second little girl. Much prayer and perseverance were sent up hoping the adoption agency would allow them to have both babies. Nevertheless, they were denied. Another family took the twins.

In spite of deep disappointment, their faith in God was strong, and they determined to continue to pray for the twins and their new parents. Relinquishing their desires, they rolled their hope upon the Lord. Soon, another little girl, the ideally perfect one became available and Teri and her mother flew to China to get little Aimee. What a joy and blessing this little almond-eyed angel has been to all our family. For you see Jack is my nephew and Teri is my niece.

A few weeks ago, out of a very difficult situation, Jack and Teri were able to adopt a little newborn boy whom they named Micah Caleb. A young teen had become pregnant and could not keep her baby. Mutual friends knew Jack and Teri and their desire for a second child. Another miraculous answered prayer. In God's timing and in His way, He gave them their two babies but not the ones they "thought" were to be theirs but the two that should have actually been theirs. Yes, they both can thank God for what they missed or else they would not have their two children today. "The steps of a good man are ordered by the Lord: and He delighteth in his way" (Psalm 37:23, KJV).

During my last year in high school when our senior class was planning a trip to the beach, my father refused to let me go. This denial hurt me so much that I cried and felt sorry for myself for days. I knew my father loved me, but I felt this decision was unreasonable. As it turned out, one of our classmates was killed in a car wreck and if I had been along on the trip, there is no doubt it would have probably been me. I was a close friend of the young man driving the car, and had often acted as his "counselor" when he and his girlfriend were having problems. That's exactly what my sweet classmate Louise was doing – just riding around giving him a listening ear as a good friend.

Many times after that, I was reminded, "It could have been me!" Yes, I can truly thank God for missing that trip to the beach.

It all comes down to this. Do you trust God even if He doesn't come through for you on things you think you must have? Ask yourself, "Is this just a desire? Or do I honestly need something?" God loves us enough to meet our genuine needs but only withholds the things we think we want, only in order to give us something for better.

- "As for God, His way is perfect" (Psalm 18:30, NIV).
- "The blessings of the Lord bring wealth, and He adds no trouble to it" (Psalm 10:22, NIV).
- "For I know the plans I have for you," declares the Lord, plans to prosper you and not to harm you, plans to give you hope and a future" (Jeremiah 29:11, NIV).

God can Build with Burned Stones

During the time God's servant Nehemiah was in the process of rebuilding his beloved Jerusalem, his enemies laughed as they watched him gather the burned and scarred stones of the city wall. "Can they bring the stones back to life from those heaps of rubble-burned as they are" (Nehemiah 4:2b)? Even as they jeered him, he was patiently gathering those discarded stones to restore the wall of the city. Not only did he attempt to build it back, but he and his fellow Jews completely restored the wall and set every gate in place. Mission accomplished, because God had chosen to do it through these men. When God plans to do something, He always succeeds. Now, of course, if He had so desired, our Heavenly Father could have had them haul stones in from any place He chose, but, instead, he built the wall back with the very stones that had been "through the fire".

There is not a one of us who have not been bruised or burned by some of life's wrong turns, our bad choices or the incorrect decisions that we, or others have made for us. Some who are the most deeply wounded, scarred or damaged can be the ones God can greatly use to "build up" His Kingdom here on earth. God has never been limited to what has happened to us or what we have done ourselves. For example, impetuous Moses killed an Egyptian who was beating one of his fellow Jews, and he was forced to go live on the backside of the desert until all of his pride and self-will was gone. Then, God used this faithful man to lead his people out of slavery. Remember Peter who lopped off the soldier's ear with a sword? Later, it was impatient Peter who denied the Lord three times. But, it was also Peter who led over 3,000 people to faith with one sermon. Paul persecuted and even killed many of the early followers of

Christ until one day he met the Lord on the road to Damascus. God used the ministry of the Apostle Paul to expand Christianity throughout the whole world.

What is the most heinous thing that you have ever done? How many people have you hurt deeply including yourself? Has God forgiven you for all of those sins? If so, why are you still grieving over your past mistakes and sins? On the other hand, who has it been that has wronged you the most in life? Have you forgiven them according to God's commandment that we have to forgive those who have deeply hurt us or sinned against us? If that is what you have done, then why are you still angry or bitter about what has happened? Evidently, some of us just refuse to believe God. If you are forgiven, God has forgotten your sin and if you have obeyed God by forgiving someone else, then, it is as if you were never sinned against. God's word says it all: "If we confess our sins, He is faithful and just and will forgive us our sins and purify us from all unrighteousness" (1 John 1:9, NIV). Did you get the last part? It means make us pure, cause us to be innocent, as if we have never sinned. If that were not true, then Jesus would have wasted His time dying on the cross. Are you a burned stone? I am. Will you allow Our Lord to say how and when He can use you to build up His kingdom? If so, there's not one thing that can stop His purposes for us. Benji Clark was taken at age 11 by her own father as his wife when Benji's mother died. Out of that brutal, hurtful past, God so healed her that today, this wonderful woman is helping thousands of young people receive God's love and restoration. Burned stones aren't blocked by pride. They just do the will of their Father.

God is a Restorer God

"David got back everything the Amalekites had taken...Nothing was missing" (1 Samuel 30:18a; 19a, NLT).

From a very early age, I was taught by my grandmother to believe God's promises in the Bible. I didn't exactly just open the Bible and point to a Scripture, but when I was really seeking an answer to some problem or needing direction in a specific undertaking, I would pick up God's word and read until I found a verse that I could count as my own. Many times, I couldn't discover a passage the first time I tried. It was always after prayer that I'd find just the right verse. By reading it over and over, I would usually be assured it was mine to claim for that particular situation.

Every morning before going to work, I would have my quiet time and Bible reading outside on our covered patio. I always drank my coffee and usually ate a piece of toast while I prayed. The Bible and my prayer journal were always left on the side table next to my patio chair in case I had time in the afternoon to pray more.

One day I returned home to discover my Bible was missing. Our children helped me look all over the house just in case I had forgotten and had carried it inside instead of leaving my Bible in its usual place, but it was no where to be found.

This particular Bible had been my favorite one because I had written so many notes about answered prayers in the margins that I grieved over my loss. I couldn't imagine where it could be. One afternoon, my Bible reading took me to the story of David's plight at Ziglag when he returned from battle. The Amalekites had burned his home, robbed his household and captured his entire family, as well as the families of all his fighting men. David was in desperate straits. In 1 Samuel 30, his men even turned against him and threatened to stone him. As I read on, I saw that that was not the end of the story. God in his mercy allowed David to recover all that was taken from him and there was nothing missing. Strange as it seems, I claimed those verses in 1 Samuel 30: 18-20.

It took one whole year, but one night I heard a knock on my back door. A lady stood there with my big black Bible in her hand. Evidently, a neighbor's big Doberman had carried it off, probably because it smelled of toast. Other that a few bite marks on certain pages, it was intact. The children in the family had decided to carry it to their church and had left it lying on the front pew of the church for all that time. I'm sure they didn't read inside and realize it was mine. Anyway, this lady had found it, saw my name and returned it. I was overjoyed.

That verse has continued to work for me in many other instances as well. Once before the elections of 2000, I believe God had given me insight as to some specific things that were taking place at the time. As usual, I wrote everything down in my prayer journal only to have it go missing too. Next, my little granddaughter's diary that I have kept on my grandchildren which documents all the fun things we have done with them and records the cute expressions they have said through the years. On the front of Cassidy's book was a porcelain cat, and she liked for me to read to her from "her" book. Then, it went missing. So, I prayed, reminding Our Father that He knew where both were and that He allowed David to "recover all" so I believed He would help me. My husband and I searched the entire house to no avail. Weeks and weeks passed but we never found either one of the missing books. One afternoon, Jerome decided to "straighten" up our grandchildren's toy box. Suddenly, he hollered to me, "Honey, I found a green book; is this Cassidy's?"

It wasn't, but it was my prayer journal. Why it was there, I'll never know. Nevertheless, its recovery was an exciting event.

Then an even more exciting thing happened the very next morning when my husband went to pick up the children to take them to school and found, just inside the door on a chair, little Cassidy's diary with the porcelain cat on the cover. When he asked her why she had carried it to her house, she answered, "Because it was mine!" Faithfully, God had allowed me to recover all that was lost.

I believe that there are many spiritual principles in God's promises that we can pray and believe God for incredible results. I shared this with a co-worker who had lost one of her diamond stud earrings. It had been a gift of love from her husband after Laura had recovered from ovarian cancer. We prayed about it and claimed God's promise of recovery. Immediately, the thought came to me that it was probably in her car. It wasn't, but later she found it in her young son's toy car inside his toy box where she obviously had dropped it while gathering up his scattered toys. Laura was astounded.

Just yesterday, I had again been claiming "recovery" for my lost I.D. tag that allowed me entrance into the T.V. Station where I work. Already, I had retraced all my stops before the I.D. had slipped off my key ring, but to no avail. In praying, I simply asked, "God, it's up to You. If it is your will, I'll recover it. If not, I will praise You anyway because You are good, all the time!" That was my last words as I waited for someone to let me in the door to our building. I looked up, and there stood my secretary grinning with my I.D. badge in her hand. Someone had mailed it in!

God is a restorer God. He cares about everything in our lives from the big tremendous conflicts to the very small things like lost Bibles, prayer journals, little girls' diaries, diamond stud earrings and I.D. Badges. Nothing is too big for Him to answer and nothing too small for Him to care about. We are His children, just like the Psalmist David, and we are loved just like he was.

Better Wronged Than Bitter

"For if you forgive men when they sin against you, your Heavenly Father will also forgive you" (Matthew 6:14, NIV).

The young woman had already been scheduled to do an interview with me on my television program. It was a known fact that she had wanted my job and in truth had said many unkind things about me to more than one person. I knew I couldn't do the interview without being a hypocrite.

Hurrying to the bathroom, I prayed for God to tell me what to do. My Co-Host, Tony, volunteered to do the interview so I wouldn't have to. By the time the show started, my guest was not there. Fifteen minutes later, I looked up to see her sneak in behind the curtain.

I looked at her then and an amazing thing happened. She looked terrified, and her make- up was almost comical in an obvious attempt to look "glamorous." All of a sudden I felt the greatest sense of liquid love pour over me for this person. The interview went off without a hitch, and I was no longer bound by an unforgiving heart. God moved!

God severs the bonds of an unforgiving heart with His healing love.

God is Always Right on Time

Be sure of this, God's timing is always perfect. When we are going through a particularly dark time in our lives, we can't see why God won't answer our prayers as quickly as we think that He should. It is very difficult to continue to have faith when delays occur. At this point, there are many people who lose hope and become bitter. There are others who choose to trust Him no matter what. If God has given you a promise, He will bring it to pass.

John and Margaret Downs found themselves in a very serious circumstance once. John had purchased a business that was similar to the one he already owned. In the past, John had always been able to successfully manage any operation that he was involved with. For some reason, nothing seemed to work in this new business. Soon, he was losing a great deal of money every month. Advisors told him to shut it down, but he just couldn't leave so many workers without a job. There just didn't seem to be a way out even though the new business endangered all of the other family holdings. John walked the floor at night praying for God to show him what to do.

One night, Margaret shared how, "John just sat straight up in bed. He heard God say to him, 'In my timing.' It gave John peace and he immediately went back to sleep. The very next day, he began to think of other companies in the "steel pole" business and decided to call one of them to see if they might possibly be interested in buying him out. When he talked to the son of one of the owners, the man said to John, "This has got to be perfect timing. My father just told me today to look for a business like this one to buy or to find some land to build one on since our business is in need of expanding." In a short time, John sold him the business and still marvels at God's timely intervention.

In our own life, my husband and I have been praying for something that we truly believe is God's will for our life, but so far, every opportunity has passed us by. My friend Rhoda recently shared a passage of Scripture with me. It was the angel Gabriel's response to Daniel. "Do not be afraid, Daniel, for from the first day that you set your heart to understand, and to humble yourself before your God, your words were heard" (Daniel 10:12, NKJV). That was the day Daniel saw his deliverance. It had been on its way all along. God has already heard the cries for help and He will answer you right on time.

Alexander Maclaren has said: "There are no 'too lates' with Him." Just remember that Jesus stayed on two more days where he was when he heard that his friend Lazarus was sick. By the time he got there, Lazarus was dead. Jesus said that this had happened for God's glory. Telling the people to roll away the stone blocking the tomb, Jesus said "Lazarus, come out" (John 11:43). The man who had been dead walked out.

God will act on your behalf just in time. He won't be one second early or one second late. He already has the solution to your present situation. He loves you enough to wait until it is the very best time to move on your behalf. One day, you will understand why He delayed. You aren't dead yet. Just wait, trust and see Him work.

God is Calling for Gatekeepers

When a gate is the only way to enter an area that gate has to be firm and secure. Those who are allowed to come in by that entrance are always the ones who have some right to enter in. Today, more than ever before God is calling for Christians to stand guard and protect what is rightfully theirs and more importantly, what is the perfect will of God. It is so easy for us to panic over the situations going on in our country. However, the best way to avoid fear and anxiety is to commit oneself to standing firm in our faith.

"For the eyes of the Lord run to and fro throughout the whole earth, to show Himself strong on behalf of those whose heart is loyal to Him" (2 Chronicles 16:9, NKJV). Are you a person whose heart totally belongs to the Lord? Do you still believe that nothing is impossible with our God and that at any moment He can turn our country and our lives around so that we are all lined up again according to His divine plan for America? If so, I challenge you to become a gatekeeper for the Lord.

In Ezekiel 22:30, God speaks: "And I searched for a man among them, who should build up the wall and stand in the gap before me for the land, that I should not destroy it; but I found no one" (Ezekiel 22:30, NASB). God could find no one to do what He required.

The Bible tells us that the four chief gatekeepers were in an office of trust. "And they spent the night around the house of God, because the watch was committed to them" (1 Chronicles 9:26-27, NASB). Gatekeepers hold an office of trust. God's richest treasures are protected by them, and whatever it takes, these individuals are alert night and day to protect His honor.

The U.S. Military is devoted and called to lay down their lives if necessary to protect our country. They are obviously chosen "gatekeepers" in keeping American from harm. However, even more important than those dedicated servicemen and women, we, who are called Christians, are battling an even higher war. All the forces of darkness are aimed at our country and it is up to us to make up the hedge, man the gates, and watch and pray that God would again be honored in our land. "A good man leaves an inheritance to his children's children..." I believe that means more than earthly wealth. A man who honors God establishes a legacy for his family that no evil can touch if he is steadfast in his faith.

Our challenge today is to pray more than ever before. The clock is ticking and the elections are near. Every Christian should vote after much prayer. Stand in the gap for America's future and the Godly heritage that we have all enjoyed so far.

Are you a Whistler or a Whiner?

It has been said many times over that it isn't what happens to a person but how they receive it that matters. All of us experience tough times. So, we can whistle through our rough patches or whine and complain about them. I'm not implying a person should "pucker up" to whistle in the midst of a tragedy. What I am saying is a person who can whistle in dark times is a person who has hope.

One has only to observe the little birds chirping away in times of sunshine or storm. They are daily confident because they have wings. A person who can manage to trust during the hardest of times can affect the entire atmosphere around them. Such a person is Dr. Ken Clark. In spite of losing his lovely wife after her valiant battle with cancer, Dr. Clark's faith and warm smile brightens up everyone's life around him. So, to, does famed athlete Sirhan Stacey. Thousands of young and old alike have been changed by the way he has offered encouragement to those who are hurting through sharing the story of the loss of his wife and all but one of his children in a terrible automobile wreck. His growth as a Christian is evident as he tells his story of triumph over tragedy.

On the other hand, there are people who can't go through a single day without grumbling or complaining about something. A banter of "poor me" conversations staves off friendship and drives away anyone who might want to offer a word of comfort.

A "whistler" brings cheer; a whiner promotes fear. In the book of Habakkuk, the prophet tells of the worst experiences he and the people of Israel had ever endured. Nevertheless, in Habakkuk 3:17, he chooses to put all of his confidence in God.

My husband of 35 years this month is my cheerleader. When I have almost fainted during his recent battle with his heart problems, his faith has remained strong. One day during his stay in the hospital, he called me to say, "I want to come home and get well so I can look after you."

Later, he was talking to my sister Martha on the phone and said, "You know during the entire ordeal I've never once been afraid of dying." I'm happy today that it is because he knows whose he is and where he would be going when he leaves this present world. My husband Jerome has never been a "whiner."

I do catch myself whining sometimes but I choose not to continue doing it. As an act of my will, I am going to be a "whistler," and in so doing, I believe I will be pleasing to my Heavenly Father.

Check it out. The next time you see someone passing through a difficult time ask yourself "Is he a "whistler" or a "whiner?" Believe me, you'll know the difference immediately.

- "Though there are no sheep in the pen and no cattle in the stalls, yet I will rejoice in the Lord, I will be joyful in God my Savior" (Habakkuk 3: 17b-18, NIV).
- "Through Jesus, therefore, let us continually offer to God a sacrifice of praise" (Hebrews 13:15, NIV).
- "and do not grumble, as some…" (I Corinthians 10:10, NIV).
- "Stop grumbling among yourselves…" (John 6:43, NIV).
- "…you have ordained praise…" (Psalm 8:2, NIV).
- "I will extol the Lord at all times; His praise will always be on my lips" (Psalm 34:1, NIV).

God is Calling for Like-minded Men

The first night our son, Trant, joined us at Providence Christian School to see our grandson, Nick, play football, he was so impressed with the new stadium there. Trant said, "Mom, it's amazing what can be accomplished by like-minded men." That statement reminded me of the call God makes for His children to "be of one mind" and to "walk in unity." "Now may the God of patience and comfort grant you to be like-minded toward one another, according to Christ Jesus, that you may with one mind and one mouth glorify the God and Father of our Lord Jesus Christ" (Romans 15:5, NKJV).

The recent elections and football season both have a lot in common. Voters with one mind turned out to elect their candidates and some amazing things happened in our country. Also, on any given week-end, high school and college teams vie for support from their fans. One thing is for sure and certain; there is a joining of minds when one team that we love clashes with another team. We, like-minded in our desires, hope and pray for the big win. If only this spirit could be carried over to our Christian faith. We pull for our candidates in political races and our football teams with absolute devotion and fervor, how much more should we strive for the salvation of souls?

Neil Anderson, engineer, author, and dedicated Bible teacher, tells of his effort to witness to a crowd of unruly teens. The obvious leader of the pack irritated Anderson more than any of the others. At each statement Neil made, the young man popped back with a question. Fighting the urge to leave or to accost the unruly youth, the man held firm to his mission and began to lovingly answer the questions that had been so rudely proposed to him. Well, the rest of the story reveals how God works in the lives of faithful Christians. That same rebellious gang leader is today Neil Anderson's beloved son-in-law and the father of his grandchildren. Yes, with Christ's love and compassion, even the seemingly hopeless cases can be won. Anderson's patience paid off and he eventually led his future son in law to Christ.

The possibilities, not the mere appearances can bring great Glory to God. For example, in a huge church one Sunday morning just as the Pastor had started his sermon, a rag-tag "hippie" barefoot and unshaven, came striding down the center aisle of that church. Seeing no place to sit, he just plopped down in the center aisle right in front of the preacher. As the congregation stared at the man, not knowing what to do, an aged usher, who was crippled and walked with a cane, came hobbling down the aisle towards the intruder. The crowd began to wonder what the elderly gentleman was going to do. Would he simply ask the unkempt man to leave or to move elsewhere? Soon, the question was answered. With great effort, because of his disability, the kindly old man slowly stooped down and sat down beside the young visitor. A dropped pin could have been heard in the church as silence reigned, until the minister stopped in the middle of his message and stated: "Ladies and gentlemen, all of you who are here today will go home and probably not remember much of what I am saying today, but I can promise you, none of you will ever forget what you have just seen here this morning."

We ought to be like-minded in spirit, in vision and in love towards God and each other in the body of Christ, so that we might win just one more. Jesus shed His blood so we have a reason to be like-minded. "If you have any encouragement from being united with Christ, if any comfort from his love, if any tenderness and compassion, then make my joy complete by being like-minded, having the same love, being one in spirit and purpose" (Philippians 2:1-2, NIV).

Do not Fear, God can Send in His Carts

      A few weeks ago, I had the privilege of speaking to a group of ladies at the Ozark Country Club at the invitation of my friend, Betty Gilland. I had two different messages prepared but decided at last on the topic, "How do you Live When You Face the Death of a Dream?" Most of us have experienced a time when we felt that God had made a promise to us concerning something dear to our hearts. Then, when we had least expected it that desired thing simply came to an end. Perhaps it was a marriage that you had believed would last for a lifetime. Or, a job you had put your faith in to see you through to old age. Whatever the dream or desire, more often than not, in this life, things are subject to change. Many times, we have to die to our dreams.

      When those times come, we have to trust in God with all our hearts. Abraham had to trust God when he faced the death of his promised son Issac. God had specifically said that it would be through Issac that all the nations of the earth would be blessed. But, Abraham was commanded to go to a mountain in the land of Moriah and offer his son as a burnt offering to the Lord. Can you imagine a more difficult thing to do? In obedience, Abraham proceeded, but just as he was preparing to kill his son, God stopped him. Abraham knew that if he killed his son, God would have to resurrect him if that promise was to come true. That is an example for all of us who are believers to follow. When we can't understand, we are to go on believing that we are greatly loved by Our Father and He knows what He is doing. If our dream dies, God can bring it back to life or give us something far better.

The very night that I had spoken to the group in Ozark, my husband and I had a crisis to face not unlike that which I have been talking about. What were we to do? We sat down, held hands and we prayed. It was very hard but we determined that in this life our hopes could not be placed in anything other than in our God. No business, person or plan could be our source of relief. Only God could provide for us. Afterwards, we both knew it was in God's hands.

A few days after our prayer together, I was reading our daily Bible selection and something jumped out at me. In Genesis 45, beginning in verse 19, the ruler of all Egypt sent Joseph back to the land of Canaan with "carts" loaded down with provisions for his needy family members. Pharaoh also offered to give them a place to live and everything else they needed. As I read those verses, the thought came to me that God could provide "carts" for us to meet our needs. The verse was so alive in my spirit that I began to praise God for sending us the "carts" or provisions we needed at this time.

Creative ideas began to come into our minds as God made us aware of provisions that He had already arranged for us long before we had faced this crisis. His timing was perfect! Jerome and I became of one mind and acted in one accord. God not only had those "carts" of provisions for us at this present time, but I know that He will continue to provide what we need until we go to be with Him in Heaven one day. Do you believe He can provide for you? He is willing if you will turn to Him in faith. "So do not fear, for I am with you; do not be dismayed, for I am your God. I will strengthen you and help you; I will uphold you with my righteous right hand" (Isaiah 41:10, NIV).

God is Forever the Hound of Heaven!

Her name is Pearl. She showed up in our yard one day life-weary and pregnant. Soon her six pups were born under our porch. As they got older Pearl watched from a distance as we took special care of her offspring. My husband and I have tried patiently to pet her but so far she has never allowed any of us to come near her. We really want to take Pearl to our vet so she can get some much needed medical care but when we try, she runs away and hides. If we could only show her that we care for her and want only to look after her and keep her safe, but of course, there is no way we can communicate that to her. Because she has evidently been abused, she is still very afraid of us.

Our interaction with Pearl reminds me of the poem "The Hound of Heaven" by Francis Thompson. In his old English terminology he writes:"I fled Him, down the nights and down the days; I fled, down the arches of the years; I fled Him, down the labyrinthine ways of my own mind: and in the mist of tears I hid from Him." It is only toward the end of the poem that the writer expresses his new understanding that it was a kind and merciful God who was chasing him and not some vicious animal or hound who would mangle and destroy him.

Aren't we all a lot like that man? We are afraid to turn our lives over to the Lord because we feel that we will be forced to do something that we don't want to do like being sent as a missionary to the darkest part of the jungles or worse still, as our friend Dudley Hall once said, "I feared God would require me to marry that very unattractive girl who had a crush on me."

Not so, as gospel songwriter and singer Walter Wilson explains. Surrendering to God was the best thing that ever happened to him. Wilson, a custodian at Bethel Baptist Church sings about his journey far away from the Lord as he struggled to resist the call of the Holy Spirit. In his early 30's, Walter finally gave up and allowed the "Hound of Heaven" to catch up with him.

Just like our stray dog Pearl, we can run, but one day His loving breath will breathe down on our necks and whisper "You belong to me!" And, when He does, you will experience the depths of His great love for us all. "For he chose us in him before the creation of the world" (Ephesians 1:4, NIV). God has a purpose for His children. He "saved us and called us to a holy life---not because of anything we have done but because of his own purpose and grace. This grace was given us in Christ Jesus before the beginning of time" (2 Timothy 1:9, NIV).

God is Never a Co-Pilot

Today, men are in desperate times. Jobs are being lost and finances are dwindling. Marriages are in trouble and young people are losing direction. Yet, according to God's word, He is still in control. Some people hang up signs or post them as bumper stickers on their cars: "God is My Co-Pilot." Sorry about that. A Co-Pilot sits by and is there only when the real Pilot needs him. With God, He is absolutely in charge all the time. This became a living reality to me years ago when I was unsure what to do with my life. I had suffered with lupus and was physically and emotionally drained. I had little financial resources, and I was back in Geneva living with my parents. One night I prayed for God to please give me some hope and, more importantly, for him to show me what to do next. He did.

That night in a dream, I found myself driving an old Model T car that was literally falling apart. As I tried to steer the car over some very dangerous roads that passed by deep valleys Model T was heading always over the edge. Try as I might, I could not control it. Then, somehow, I gave up and lay back against the back of the seat taking my hands completely off the steering wheel. Immediately, I found myself in my father's big white 98' Oldsmobile with his power steering moving the wheel. I was elated! Wow, I knew I could drive now with my Dad's big powerful Olds. I placed my hands, enthusiastically, on the steering wheel and poof, I was somehow back in that rickety old car and this time I was truly headed over the cliff. I must have yelled in the dream and quickly "took my hands off" the controls. That was all it took. I found myself back in my father's car completely safe and at ease. The car was continuing down the road with absolutely no help from me.

When I woke up the next morning, I knew what God had been trying to tell me. When I tried to control my life, I was failing and also running into danger, but when I totally released the controls, My Father was the pilot. What a wonderful blessing that dream was for me. I immediately got down on my knees and thanked God for His plan for my life, and I promised to trust Him to show me what to do next. It was not long before I had clear direction for the next step in my life. And, by the way, it worked out wonderfully well as does all of God's plans for His children.

I really don't know why God gave me that wonderful dream that night. Maybe He knew how desperate I was at the time. He doesn't always speak to me like that, but He is faithful to show up when He is needed the most. His Word speaks to us. Just remember God's promise to us. "For I am the Lord, your God, who takes hold of your right hand and says to you, Do not fear, I will help you" (Isaiah 41:13, NIV). And ultimately, we should always be reminded: "In his heart a man plans his course, but the Lord determines his steps" (Proverbs 16:9, NIV).

Being Punished When you are Innocent

When I was in the fourth grade, I received a lick with a paddle on my open palm. I had done nothing wrong, and I knew it. Tears stung my eyes as I returned to my seat. It was the first and the only 'paddling' I ever received in school. Our teacher had left the room for about twenty minutes and threatened to paddle us all if we misbehaved. Only two boys said anything while she was gone. The rest of us didn't say a word. We all got spanked anyway. It was unfair then, and something like that is still unfair today. I was so glad my father didn't also spank me at home as he had always said he would do if I got in trouble at school. Thankfully, he understood I was innocent and had been punished when I didn't deserve it.

Years ago my friend Dick Teipel told us about a spanking he had given one of his daughters right after he had returned home from Vietnam. His youngest child had started escaping from her baby bed at night. Nothing seemed to work to keep her in bed. He and his wife were afraid Karen would hurt herself in some way. She was also good about taking the chain locks off and had managed, on one occasion, to get outside before they caught her.

One night, in desperation, he had told her that if she climbed out one more time, she was going to get the spanking of her life. Later, when everyone had gone to bed, he woke up to hear little feet running down the hall. He jumped up, and in the dark, grabbed his child and began to spank her. She was yelling, but he couldn't understand her until his wife cut the lights on. To his surprise, he was spanking the wrong child. Karen had managed to get out of her crib all right, but it had been Kathy who had run down the hall to tell on her sister when Dick had grabbed her thinking she was her younger sister. Kathy had been innocent, but she was punished anyway.

Then, I remember the time when my cousin's husband, Glen Wise, had spanked their daughter Laura for jabbing holes into a leather hassock. He probably would not have spanked her if she had been willing to admit her guilt. Over and over he had asked her why she had done this, and every time she had answered that she hadn't done it. Even after he spanked her, she was still proclaiming her innocence. Laura was so hurt with her father that Glen began to question why she wouldn't admit her guilt.

Later, when their maid was cleaning up Laura's closet she found a cardboard box with holes punched all through it. When she showed it to the child's mother, Sara knew exactly what had happened. After this, the parents showed Laura the box and she readily admitted that she had punched holes through the box. She had not realized that she had, inadvertently, also punched holes in the leather foot rest when she had placed the box on top of it to steady her project. That's why she protested her innocence; because she had no idea the holes had been punched all the way through to the leather foot rest. She was innocent of not 'deliberately' punching those holes in valuable furniture.

All of these incidents are absolutely true and so is the punishment of the only truly innocent person that ever lived— the Lord Jesus Christ. Never forget that when you are falsely accused or may have to pay for something that you haven't done. Most importantly, the death of this perfect man made it possible for all who receive him to be forgiven of every wrong doing they have ever done and be able to receive eternal life as well.

Even though the Lord Jesus Christ was not guilty of sin "he was pierced for our transgressions, he was crushed for our iniquities; the punishment that brought us peace was upon him, and by his wounds we are healed. We all, like sheep have gone astray, each of us has turned to his own way; and the LORD has laid on him the iniquity of us all" (Isaiah 53:5-6, NIV).

God Promises His Blessings Even as we Grow Older

Some of the greatest stories of success came about after a person was well into old age. Most people are familiar with the founder of the Kentucky Fried Chicken franchise. That is why the picture of Colonel Sanders is depicted on all the advertisements with his grey hair and beard. Then, there is the artist Grandma Moses who was not discovered until she was well into her 90's.

Author James Michener never had a book published until he decided to self-publish in his forties. After the Hearst foundation purchased the rights to "The Bridge on Toko-Ri", Michener was prolific in his writing until he died at a ripe old age.

If you had a dream in your youth that has never been fulfilled, in God's economy, it is never too late to accomplish the desire of your heart.

My dentist and friend, Dr. Labruce Hanahan, chuckles about his practicing dentistry way past the time he could have chosen to retire. "Why should I retire" he quipped, "I sit around all day practicing my craft, talk to my friends and some of them even pay me a little money every now and then. I wouldn't do that well in a nursing home."

Gynecologist Dr. Clyde Smith enjoys his medical practice so much that he intends to continue helping his women patients stay healthy until he is no longer able to work.

Jacquie Moore is doing her best work now that she has "retired" from the Dothan Country Club. Her expertise is much in demand as a wedding planner and catering consultant.

Each of these learned to trust in God who promises that we will be able to continue on and do great exploits even in our old age. I especially believe this for myself. I believe because of the testimony of Scripture.

- And now, in my old age, don't set me aside. (Psalm 71:9, NLT)
- Now that I am old and gray,...Let me proclaim your power to this new generation, your mighty miracles to all who come after me. (Psalm 71:18, NLT)
- Even in old age they will still produce fruit; they will remain vital and green. (Psalm 92:14, NLT)
- The glory of the young is their strength; the gray hair of experience is the splendor of the old. (Proverbs 20:29, NLT)
- I will be your God throughout your lifetime – until your hair is white with age. I made you, and I will care for you. I will carry you along and save you. (Isaiah, 46:4, NLT)

How to Stop Pointing the Finger

I attended the Healthy Woman Seminar sponsored by Enterprise Medical Center. The guest speaker, Lisa Smart, was a gifted and comedic spokesperson. Her hilarious stories brought the house down with peals of laughter. However, in the midst of all her joking, she made two very specific points! (How I wish I had come up with these significant directives.) "One," she said, "is never, never be guilty of pointing the finger" or in other words practicing judging others.

To illustrate this statement, she humorously explained that she had always been able to stay within her budget. On the other hand, over-eating was the bane of her existence. Therefore, when a young woman came to ask counsel from Lisa one day because she was $3,000.00 in debt on her credit card, frugal Lisa wanted to command: "If you can't afford it, don't buy it!" But, just as she was about to express this, God spoke to her: "If you aren't hungry, don't eat that second 'Little Debbie' bar!"

The entire audience cracked up at that, but the speaker went on to quietly say that "pointing the finger," judging and/or gossiping are just as wrong as the one caught up in excess or sin of any kind. Because all of us are imperfect beings who are full of faults that need to be corrected, we should be more compassionate toward others.

The alternative to "pointing the finger," Ms. Smart explained, is to "put your arm around that troubled person and to come along side of them to offer them true, loving help." Those who suffer from any form of addiction, even those who can't refrain from gossiping need vital support to overcome these problems.

Lisa Smart didn't say this, but it seems very appropriate at this time to mention that when a person is "pointing the finger" at someone, the very posture of the hand causes the other appendages to point right back at the pointer!

Remember the story in the Bible recorded in John chapter eight when a woman caught in adultery was brought to Jesus to be judged. The law was clear. She was to be stoned. Jesus, however, bent down and began writing in the dirt, then he said, "If any of you is without sin, let him be the first to throw a stone at her" (John8:7, NIV). As he continued to write, one by one from the oldest to the youngest, they began to leave. To prove that just because Jesus didn't condemn the woman, he certainly didn't condone her sin, he said to her when she saw no one was left to accuse her "Go now and leave your life of sin" (John 8:11, NIV).

That's the bottom line, we are never to condone sin but at the same time, we are not supposed to be guilty of condemning the sinner. All of us take pride in our strengths while attempting to cover our weaknesses. The only possible way to alleviate out flaws, however, is to admit them and seek help to overcome these areas of our failures.

God loves us enough to tell us in His word: "Do not judge and you will not be judged. Do not condemn, and you will not be condemned. Forgive, and you will be forgiven" (Luke 6:37, NIV).

In essence, stop the pointing of the finger in judgment at others. Then, determine to come along side of our fellow strugglers and help them to get well. In so doing, we will truly be finding special assistance for our own ills.

Hope for Those Who've Been Sinned Against

I received an e-mail from a woman who had read my article on the stain of sin. She asked me several questions. "What about the people who are left with a stain? What about the children who are victims of abuse, alcoholic parents, violence, etc.? How do you remove a stain that is poured on you from birth and continues as an adult?"

There is no perfect response to her plea, but since I believe God is a restorer God, there has to be a way to overcome the pain that still remains long after the sin was actually committed. Because the victim is still suffering, that person remains in bondage to the sin that was done against them. It is God's will to set them free!

True healing of the memories is possible only through trust in God and being willing to forgive whoever sinned against you. The memory of the events will always remain but without the pain associated with them. I know it is possible because of many different testimonies of people who have been restored.

The author of "There's an Elephant in My Living Room" tells how the memory of a rape by a camp counselor when she was only 12 had affected all areas of her life. However, God showed her how to be delivered from that hurt forever. The same thing happened for a pastor's wife who had been molested over a period of years by her own father. Both of these women were finally able to forgive the person responsible for their pain. Today they are set free of guilt or shame.

The total delivery from those painful traumas in our past can only be accomplished when one comes to the realization that it was not their fault that they became victims. Next, they have to release all anger toward God and toward the one or ones who victimized them. Ask God to help you forgive those who have deeply hurt you. Resist the temptation to blame yourself for not being able to stop what happened to you. Then pray and completely submit to our loving heavenly Father. Listen to these words from the inspired prophet Jeremiah. "For I know the plans I have for you, says the lord. They are plans for good and not for evil, to give you a future and a hope. In those days when you pray, I will listen. You will find me when you seek me, if you look for me in earnest. Yes, I will be found by you, and I will end your slavery, and restore your fortunes" (Jeremiah 29:11-14, LB).

If God is willing to forgive the guilty person when he repents, how much more is he willing to heal the innocent person who was sinned against?

God Still knows who you Are

A few days ago, I read an article about a man who had lost his job and then was re-educated to work in a completely different field. This individual was totally lost and confused. As he stated in the article: "I no longer know who I am. All of this is completely foreign to me. In my old job, I was comfortable because I knew what kind of person I was; now, I am not sure."

As I look around, I am aware of many other people struggling with the same identity crisis. It seems that there are a large number of folks feeling like their true identity has been stolen. It may be because of a lost position, a divorce, an economic reversal or even the death of a spouse. Truth be told, all of us are guilty to a certain extent of thinking of ourselves in certain set ways, such as, "I am a doctor, or I am a teacher." Or, I am "Mrs. John Smith" or "we live in a gated community." When life changes occur, and they always do, those statements may not be true any longer. If that happens, then, how can one define who he is?

To answer simply, for those of us who are in Christ Jesus, our identity comes from knowing that we are a child of God. Jesus has committed himself to us, and nothing can ever separate us from His love and care. We must take comfort in God's counsel. "Though I walk in the midst of trouble, You will revive me; You will stretch forth Your hand against the wrath of my enemies, and your right hand will save me. The Lord will perfect that which concerns me; Your mercy and loving kindness, O Lord, endure for ever; forsake not the works of Your own hands" (Psalm 138:7-8). God's Word not only gives us counsel, it gives us encouragement. "And I am convinced and sure of this very thing, that He Who began a good work in you will continue until the day of Jesus Christ" (Philippians 1:6, The Amplified Bible).

You may think that God has forgotten you or changed His mind about what He had intended for your life, but that is simply not so. If there has been a sudden change in the circumstances in your life, then, He is preparing you for something far better. Jeremiah 29:11 is one of my all time very Bible verses because the Lord Himself promises: "For I know the thoughts and plans that I have for you, says the Lord, thoughts and plans for welfare and peace, and not for evil, to give you hope in your final outcome" (The Amplified Bible). So, don't be afraid, God still knows who you are even if you don't. If you will trust in Him and be willing to "wear the hat" that He is presently calling upon you to wear, then, your end will always be successful and will ultimately bring great glory to the Lord. There is always the "afterwards" of His gracious Promising.

God Still Sits as King Over the Flood

Grief can come like a dark torrent of epic proportions. The thing you most feared has happened. When a loved one dies, a flood of sorrow can overwhelm a person. The pain grips you immediately and there seems to be no let-up. Yet, the good news is that God has made a way in the midst of these difficult circumstances so that we can endure and make it through these times. It is the promise we can hold on to as we celebrate the birth of the Christ Child.

In the space of just a few short months, we have lost three loved ones to cancer. First, we lost my sister's husband Howard. A few months later we lost our dear godly friend Melinda Jones. Then just weeks later the director of my TV shows, Joe Holloway, also succumbed to cancer. We can question the question "why" and stay in deep depression or we can lift our eyes toward Heaven and receive God's peace. As the waves of sadness threaten to engulf us, we need only to remember that because of the birth of the Christ child, there is always hope of the "afterwards of His gracious promising." This life is not the end. When Jesus died on the cross for the sins of the world, He made a way for us to walk with Him for all eternity. One day, for those of us who have received the gift of salvation, we will see our loved ones again.

When darkness rolls over us like a flood, we can remember the inspired words from the Psalmist. "He stilled the storm to a whisper; the waves of the sea were hushed" (Psalm 107:29, NIV). It is all because of Jesus that we can have the hope of a better tomorrow. We can know without a doubt that this world is not the end. Ultimately, we can become like the person described in the Word of God. "He will have no fear of bad news; his heart is steadfast, trusting in the Lord" (Psalm 112:7, NIV).

American military hero Major General Bill Brown died on Thanksgiving Day. One of his greatest accomplishments was heading up the campaign that ultimately freed the prisoners of war in Viet Nam. His widow, Ann, told me that the memorial service for him December 18th in Santa Rosa Beach would include a "fly-over" by the military to honor his memory. His heart had simply given out as he battled pneumonia. Another tragic loss. But then, the Creator of all mankind has a continuing plan for those who have gone on before us. Even though we can't imagine how we can live without those we love, our place is to trust Him to daily give us His grace to continue on. I truly believe that if any of these wonderful people I have mentioned had a choice, they would never return to this life no matter how much they loved us. They have simply moved to a better location and they are, I believe, rejoicing as they wait for us to follow.

In Christ, we are "Prisoners of Hope!"

As we are entering a new year, it is evident that we will be facing many serious challenges. There is a wall of uncertainty out there and none of us have a handle on just what we might have to deal with in 2011. However, for those of us who have put our entire trust in Christ, we can walk through the next year with hope in our hearts because of "Who He is" and "Who we are in Him."

While reading my Bible a few days ago, I came across a marvelous Scripture in the book of Zechariah. "Return to your fortress, O prisoner of hope; even now I announce that I will restore twice as much to you" (Zechariah 9:12). As I thought about this verse, I was reminded how many times I had come to a so-called dead end in my life, only to see how good God was to open yet another window. In all my years of walking with Him, He has never failed me yet.

Imagine a young soldier lying on the battlefield seriously wounded knowing that since all the Medi-Vac helicopters had obviously been ordered out due to the heavy artillery, there was no hope that you would ever live to see your family and home again, Then, you hear it. It is the sound of another helicopter, a big Huey being flown by someone who was not called to do this. Captain Ed Freeman flew in 13 times until all the wounded were rescued even though he sustained four hits to his legs and left arm. He received the Medal of Honor for his heroism that day from the U.S. Air Force, but that was not why this soldier did what he did. He flew in the face of severe machine gun fire risking his own life and the helicopter he flew because that was the right thing to do. Twenty nine young men lived that day because of the bravery of one of their own. Every time that Huey landed, the men on the ground yelled out with joy. They could not move but their hope was secure. That's the way I think it is to be "prisoners of hope." There is nothing we can do because we are pinned down in some situation or other, but then our God swoops down and takes us up in His Loving Care and rescues His own.

There was not much hope left for the family of Bryan Hall one night when a severe asthmatic attack led to full pulmonary arrest. Often the monitor had flat-lined and at one point air had leaked out into his chest cavity so much that his body blew up like a balloon. The doctors inserted bilateral chest tubes to relieve it.

Bryan writes: "On the seventh night, my family was told again I wouldn't make it through the night. My sister, Patsy, however, had other ideas and brought Miss Ann in to pray over me. I was in a medically induced coma, but I remember Miss Ann praying and I understood every word of it. I was given a very simple choice that night. Accept Jesus Christ as your Savior or your journey ends here. I made that choice and now I believe that God did nothing for me that night that he wouldn't do for anyone if you asked him to. It doesn't matter what you have done or not done. God's grace forgives all who ask to be forgiven. I will guarantee you that your life will change."

Bryan Hall lives today because of Who made him a "prisoner of hope". It is the same Holy Spirit that is waiting for you to come and invite Him into your life as your Lord and Savior. If you do, I promise you, He will grant you so much more than you have ever had before. "He fulfills the desires of those who fear him; he hears their cry and saves them" (Psalm 145:19, NIV).

501063

CUSTOMER'S ORDER NO.				DATE	6. 8 11	
NAME						
ADDRESS						
CITY, STATE, ZIP						

SOLD BY	CASH	C.O.D.	CHARGE	ON. ACCT.	MDSE. RETD.	PAID OUT

QUAN.	DESCRIPTION		PRICE	AMOUNT	
1	1	ANN VANNum		7	ore
2					
3					
4					
5					
6					
7					
8					
9					
10					
11					
12					

RECEIVED BY

A-4705
F-46528

KEEP THIS SLIP FOR REFERENCE

01-11

God Thinks About you all the Time

In an age when everyone is looking for love and acceptance, there is only one sure way to know true affirmation. Let me explain why I believe this is true.

Her name is Sandy and she has taught children in an old-fashioned "Dames School" for over twenty years. The concept is really more familiar in the mid-western states where classes are conducted in the home of an educated neighbor, much in the same way a "home school" is held. Neighborhood children come to the school for three or four hours a day and then their parents teach some of the subjects at home.

One day, Sandy began realizing that in her effort to stay on top of her class work and also take care of her own family, she had totally neglected to look after herself. In other words, she was overweight, her hair was a mess, and her choice of clothing caused her to look incredibly "frumpy".

Deciding to change her looks, she set out on a "make-over." She started on a daily exercise program, had her hair styled in an easy to keep new do, and bought a few new "more youthful" outfits. Daily, she rose earlier, and even began wearing make-up and light fragrance. One morning as she viewed herself in the mirror, she thought, "Oh, Lord, I can't believe I'm thinking so much about myself lately. I feel so guilty!" Just then, she sensed a response in her spirit. "Well, I think about you all the time!" Immediately, as tears sprang to her eyes, she realized God had once again assured her of His love for her.

It is hard for us to believe that not only does God cherish us but, He desires to spend time with each one of His children. "How can this be?" Nevertheless, it is true if you believe what the Bible says about God's "always available" love. "How priceless is your unfailing love! Both high and low among men find refuge in the shadow of your wings" (Psalm 36:7, NIV).

I remember one time when we were on the way to an "out of town" Auburn football game and realized, in our rush, we had forgotten to make room reservations. It was before cell phones were in wide use. While my husband tried calling ahead on a pay phone to book a motel, I sat in the car and prayed for God to intervene in our behalf. Almost immediately, the Scripture from Isaiah came to mind. "Can a mother forget the baby at her breast and have no compassion on the child she has borne? Though she may forget, I will not forget you! See, I have engraved you on the palms of my hand" (Isaiah 49:15-16, NIV).

Moments later, we received a room since a cancellation had just been called in. If we had not stopped at that exact time, we would have missed it.

"How precious to me are your thoughts, O God! How vast is the sum of them!" (Psalm 139:17, NIV). "For I know the plans I have for you," declares the Lord, "plans to prosper you and not to harm you, plans to give you hope and a future" (Jeremiah 29: 11, NIV).

And, that, my friends, is far better than having money in the bank!

Jesus Promises Peace

A few weeks ago, I listened to a radio message by Ron Mehl, whose words live on even though he has long since been dead. It was such an encouraging lesson that I started sharing what he said with others.

Pastor Mehl explained that when the disciples came to wake the sleeping Jesus while he was taking a nap on the ship in the middle of a terrible storm, he immediately woke up and rebuked the storm commanding "Peace, be still" (Mark 4:39, NIV). The winds and the waves immediately stopped to their amazement. His followers didn't understand that Jesus (who is Peace) was there all the time and they didn't recognize it.

Later, while Jesus was still instructing those who followed him in preparation for his death on the cross, he spoke comforting words to them. "Peace I leave with you, my peace I give you. I do not give to you as the world gives. Do not let your hearts be troubled and do not let it be afraid" (John 14:27, NLB).

Just before and after this promise of his peace remaining with them, he also told them the Counselor (the Holy Spirit) would remain with them. That means the Holy Spirit lives within every believer's heart already.

Peace is not some "floating feel good" moment in time; it is Jesus, our Lord, Himself. If we have the Holy Spirit within us, then we have all the peace we'll ever need. It's just a matter of accepting that fact and relying on it.

Of course, I started telling everyone about how I had learned to always have "Peace" and that very night I was put to the test. When we got home, all three of our dogs were gone. I immediately panicked. Then, I remembered what I had been sharing with everyone about "Peace", and so I had to "practice what I had been preaching." It worked! Even though my dogs didn't come home all night, as much as I love them I knew I couldn't afford to lose my peace with their disappearance. A day and a half later they came home. It was very hard not to worry because I do love those dogs but "Peace" stayed firm. Just remember, if you belong to Him, you'll always have "Peace" if you'll just believe it.

No Good Thing Will God withhold from Me

A few weeks back on a Saturday morning while I was spending my usual prayer time, I was questioning why so many different things in my life had not worked out the way that I had hoped they would. Truthfully, I was complaining a little to the Lord that there had been times that I didn't think it was fair that my hopes had been squashed. So many times when my husband and I had truly believed a door was opened for us, that opening had been firmly slammed shut. Prayers that we had been praying for years had also never been answered. In the midst of all this, a thought of affirmation popped into my head: "No good thing will You withhold from me." It was just something I immediately knew was the absolute truth.

Since I always read through the Bible each year, I then picked up the Scripture reading for the day. The Old Testament reading in Jeremiah was all about God's anger at disobedient Israel and 2 Thessalonians spoke of God's devotion to those He chooses. The Psalm for that day was Psalm 84 and as I read verse 3 reminded me that even the sparrow and the swallow chose a nest for themselves where they could have their young near God's altar. I remembered reading that verse years ago, and by faith choosing to lay our children securely there near God's altar. Verse 5: "Blessed are those whose strength is in you...and verse 6..."passing through the valley of Baca (tough times) they make it a place of springs." Verse 7 "They go from strength to strength." Each verse being even more significant and special in my life until I reached verse 11: "For the Lord is a Sun and Shield. The lord bestows favor and honor. No good thing does He withhold from those whose walk is blameless…" Wow, God had placed the thought in my head first and then confirmed it with specific Scripture, even though I had no idea what my Bible reading for that day would be.

The truth of that Word to me was that as always God knew best, and He would always give us exactly what we needed, when we needed it and not before. When God speaks once it is wonderful, when He confirms that word with Scripture it is awesome, but when He reveals it a third time, it is a done deal. That next morning at our church, as our Associate Pastor Ron Bruce stepped up to do his usual "welcome" he explained that he just felt led to read a passage from Psalm 84,and you know the rest. He concluded with these words: "No good thing does He withhold from those whose walk is blameless." The rest of the Psalm, verse 12: "O Lord Almighty, blessed is the man who trusts in you." That's what it's all about! Our place is to TRUST Him and He will do what is best for us all.

When you Really Need a "Do Over"

Remember when we were growing up and trying our hand at some new game? No matter how hard we tried, our first attempts were often fruitless. Nevertheless, kids can be very tolerant of each other so they usually gave in when one of us begged, "I want a do over." In other words, please give me another chance to do it again. Sometimes, our "do overs" lasted a long time, but there were many times when we weren't allowed to have a second chance. It all depended on who we were playing with and whether they were friends or kin. Friends usually gave in easier that kin (especially our brothers and sisters).

Just like those fun times in our youth when we desperately needed another chance to "do it right," as adults many times we find ourselves longing to be able to start over with a clean slate. If we could only get one more chance, we believe then we'd never make the same mistakes.

My senior year at Huntingdon College in Montgomery, Alabama, I had to take volleyball as an elective PE course. The classes (at the time) were held in the basement of the boy's dormitory. I've never been a skilled athlete, but I was required to pass my PE courses even though they didn't count for college academic points.

Lobbing those volleyballs high enough to clear the net in the middle and still keep them lower than the overhead pipes and structure was not only very hard for me, but it was also terrifying. I was just not good at it period. On the day of my final test, I got twenty chances to hit the ball in certain areas of the court just over that middle volleyball net. It was a disaster!!! Try as I could, I didn't get many right. I just knew I had failed the course. Later, I returned to the dorm in total defeat. Even though I had prayed for a miracle, it just didn't happen.

On the following Monday morning, I trudged into the basement with drooping shoulders and even lower spirits. I knew my teacher was going to give us our grades and that would mean an automatic requirement to take the course again because of my failure. As we waited for our test scores, our coach got up and began explaining that somehow she had completely lost all of the test results. "I really am sorry," she continued, "but it looks like you are going to have to do the test all over again." I couldn't believe my ears but, nonetheless, it was true.

As a result of my "do over", don't ask me how (except maybe angelic intervention), I made a high A. I actually only missed one, and I managed to at least get it over the net. Wow! That was an exciting time. More than exciting, it was just an example of God's mercy to me. But then, God is a God that delights in second chances. If you don't believe it, study the genealogy of Jesus in Matthew chapter one. Every woman listed there had something bad happen in her past or she herself was guilty of wrong doing. Tamar tricked her father-in-law into committing incest. Rahab was a harlot. Bathsheba committed adultery and on and on. Ironically, the only women listed were those who had either had a shameful past or at least had been ill thought of. No other woman is listed except those that needed that second chance and God not only gave them one, but He ordered it recorded in His book of life, the Bible.

Do you need another chance right now? Maybe a "Do over" would perhaps fix things in your life? If so, just cry out to God for His forgiveness and mercy. The Prodigal son in Luke 15:11 got another chance, and you can receive one, too. Just ask Him.

In the Holy Bible, numbers have very special spiritual significance. The number eight, for example, is the number of "new beginnings." On the eighth day, Jesus rose from the dead and a new order was ushered in. For instance, eight is the number for the new birth. God loves to grant new life and a second chance to "get it right." The Bible tells us that "blessed are they whose transgressions are forgiven whose sins are covered" (Romans 4:7, NIV).

What Time I am Afraid

Recently, my friend and co-worker, Wayne Register, was facing open heart surgery. Naturally, he experienced a great deal of anxiety over what was about to happen to him. Many of his friends tried to encourage him and entire congregations in our city were praying for him. Nevertheless, I am sure he faced many fears. When we talked with him, Wayne's sweet spirit and his faith would shine through, but it was obvious that underneath his bravado, he was still deeply troubled, and who wouldn't be?

One day while he was waiting for his surgery, I dropped by with a special gift for him. It was a very long-legged stone frog who was obviously positioned in a "thoughtful" pose. "Wayne", I said, "this is Wilbur, the worry frog. Don't you worry anymore because he will do all your worrying for you!" Of course we all got a big laugh out of this. Inside a card I had placed with Wayne's "worry frog" was a short note expressing God's trustworthiness and an admonition not to fear but to turn everything over to the only One who could handle the entire situation.

On the cover of the card was a small kitty sitting propped up against a pillow in the corner of a couch, sound asleep. Now, that is a perfect picture of being so relaxed that you fall asleep in whatever position you're in. What a perfect picture of "rest" and that's truly the place God wants us to be in no matter what we're facing.

Shortly before Wayne's surgery, we had prayed with our banker Kay Thomas's Dad, James Watkins, who had also undergone open heart surgery. With only a few complications, Mr. Watkins had sailed through his ordeal. I told Wayne all about how well Kay's father had done and I reminded Wayne that he was much younger than Mr. Watkins.

Well, the surgery is behind Wayne Register now; he is home and is getting well. That is one more direct answer to many, many prayers. But, what about all the times a person doesn't make it through surgery? What happens when the diagnosis is "terminal cancer" and there doesn't appear to be any hope? Divorce is inevitable? A child is arrested for drug possession?

For those who truly believe they have a personal relationship with Christ, then the following Scriptures will be the only comfort you will need when you feel afraid for any reason.

- "When I am afraid, I will trust in you" (Psalm 56:3, NIV).
- "in God I trust; I will not be afraid. What can man do to me" (Psalm 56:11, NIV)?
- "You will not fear the terror of night, nor the arrow that flies by day" (Psalm 91:5, NIV).
- "He will have no fear of bad news; his heart is steadfast, trusting in the LORD. His heart is secure, he will have no fear; in the end he will look in triumph on his foes" (Psalm 112:7-8, NIV).

Then, Jesus Himself left us with a "forever promise."

- "Peace I leave with you; my peace I give you. I do not give to you as the world gives. Do not let your hearts be troubled and do not be afraid" (John 14:27, NIV).

To Succeed in Life - Stay Focused

In today's culture, being successful seems to be the goal of every person – especially the young. Sports figures desire fame and money based on their individual ability to perform. A master architect is striving for the "perfect" design to put him on top. The businessman is longing for the "big deal" to make his fortune and on and on.

Success may be defined in more than one way by different people. Often, an individual may believe that being successful equals being happy. Success does not necessarily bring happiness. Some of the folks the world considers the "most successful" are in truth, utterly miserable.

So, what is the bottom line? Is there something called "success" that will bring a person true happiness? And, the answer is a resounding "yes!" The way to achieve this type of success is to stay focused. Never waver, never quit and never give up. Stay the course and remain true to your dream. Don't be like my eight year old granddaughter, Cassidy, who desperately wanted to go to the beach. The only problem was that her brother's very successful baseball team kept winning their ball games so they couldn't leave town. During one of the play-off games, Cassidy and her mother stayed at home, but Cassidy kept calling us to see how the game was going. Ironically, a very good play on Nicholas's part put his team ahead and they won their game. When Nick and his Dad got home, Cassidy had written her brother this note: "Dear Nick, I hate you! Love, Cassidy."

I know that is a humorous example of being ambivalent. True success will never allow for that, as my friend, author and artist, Jeannie St. John Taylor, told her writing students after she told them about Cassidy's mixed rebuke to her brother. One must make up their mind and stay true to their belief, no matter what.

The apostle Paul defines, I believe in terms of true success. "However, I consider my life worth nothing to me, if only I may finish the race and complete the task the Lord Jesus has given me — the task of testifying to the gospel of God's grace" (Acts 20:24, NIV).

In essence, if any person has the security of having a personal relationship with his God, then his life is truly successful. Staying focused, and on course in the plan He has for our inner being the only real contentment one will ever find.

The apostle Paul concludes that he had stayed focused almost at the end of his earthly life. "I have fought the good fight, I have finished the race, I have kept the faith. Now there is in store for me the crown of righteousness, which the Lord, the righteous Judge, will award to me on that day – and not only to me, but also to all who have longed for his appearing" (2 Timothy 4:7-8, NIV).

Answer this question for yourself. Do you want true success? If so, you will find it, I believe, in only one way. You will find success by discovering God's will for your life and staying absolutely true, without hesitating to it.

Sin is Sneaky Like a Spider's Web

He smoked only one marijuana cigarette. It was the very first time he had ever smoked pot; yet, after that one "joint", he was hopelessly addicted. Why? Some very cruel drug dealer had previously laced the raw marijuana with methamphetamines. A high school student took her first drink at her senior prom. Someone had spiked it with the "date rape" drug. The young teen woke up the next morning pregnant. In an instant, just like the web of a spider, these two young people had been ensnared and bound up so tightly that their lives were being crushed. Both of these stories are true.

Lois Galloway saw firsthand a spiritual principal behind a spider's spun net. One time she was going through a very difficult time. Her "new" blended family was not what she had planned on, and she chose to return to her old family home to "think things through." As she sat on the front porch reading the newspaper, a yellow jacket came swarming near her head, so she swatted it down thinking to finish it off by stepping on the insect. Instead when she glanced down at the floor, she saw the little bug totally wrapped up in a spider's web. It had become so ensnared that even as it fought, the yellow jacket was quickly rolled up in a tiny ball and immediately snatched under the settee. As she watched this very quick "capture", she realized that just like the lightning wrap-up by the spider, Satan had been busy spinning her into confusion and deceiving her mind as to what was really important. She quickly repented and returned to her family.

Sin is insidious. Just like it can entrap a person, it can also lure someone into thinking they are safe and secure when they are anything but safe and secure. People are tempted to trust in their wealth, their business, their family, social connections or anything else except God. When trust is misplaced, devastation is inevitable. The Scripture further verifies this in Job 8:13a – 14, 15:

> Such is the destiny of all who forget God;
> What he trusts in is fragile;
> What he relies on is spider's web.
> He leans on his web, but it gives way;
> He clings to it, but it does not hold (NIV).

God's power is the only reliable source in life to protect us. His love is also the only anchor that will ultimately hold us.

- "If any lacks wisdom, he should ask God who gives generously to all without finding fault, and it will be given to him" (James 1:15, NIV).
- "Trust in the Lord and do good; dwell in the land and enjoy safe pasture. Delight yourself in the Lord and He will give you the desire of your heart" (Psalm 37:3, NIV).

Heroes in Pursuit of Happiness

Heroes come about because of extraordinary deeds performed during extremely difficult times. Anyone can become a hero. Just check the Bible. The shepherd boy David became one when he killed the giant Goliath. David did not look at the size of the Philistine who stood before him; instead, the youth looked to his God who was in control of everything.

Like David, sometimes we can face a "giant" situation in our life when we are called upon to perform a task way out of our comfort zone. Such is the case of a man I met recently named Mitch Johnson. "This man is my hero," said Dr. Tim Tucker as he introduced me to him. "I wouldn't even want to practice veterinary medicine without him. You see, Mitch Johnson took on his three children to raise all by himself when his daughter was about 6, one son was 4 and the baby boy was only 14 or 15 months old." Johnson not only had the total responsibility of caring for his three little ones, but he didn't have a baby sitter or transportation. This did not keep him from walking to work every day and carrying the children with him. His previous boss, Dr. Andrew Tamplin appreciated this faithful father and gave him his first car. Much later, when Johnson's son needed the old car to take to college, Dr. Tucker presented his friend with another car to drive.

I asked Mitch how he managed to raise three great children alone. He smiled, "One day at a time. I had a step-father who took on the care of four of us kids when he married our mother, so I figured if he could do that, then I could surely bring up my own kids."

Grinning, the tall African American gentleman admitted, when I asked, if he had seen "In Pursuit of Happiness "the movie starring Will Smith. It was about a young man who had achieved great success in the stock market while caring for his young son alone. For a long time, Smith's character didn't even have a place to live, but he managed to overcome great obstacles to achieve his goal in life. Mitch Johnson has done like-wise with God's help.

When a man like Mitch is willing to do his part, then God will certainly do His part. Another partner in the Veterinary Practice, Dr. Snell also speaks highly of Johnson. "Everyone likes him because he seems to enjoy helping others. He works hard and always cares about what he is doing."

Always faithful to carry his children to his church, Sardis Baptist Church, Johnson set the standards high for his three offspring and now, too, for his grandchildren. There are many single parents out there today, but those who turn to the Lord in their time of difficulty will find the help they need. "When anxiety was great within me, your consolation brought joy to my soul" (Psalm 94:19, NIV). Now that's a verse anyone can count on. In obedience to God, anyone can be a hero and find true happiness in this life.

Life After Rejection

Everyone knows the feeling of rejection. When my daughter was young, she always thought I loved her brother more than I loved her. Even though that was completely untrue, nevertheless, she felt that way. Sometimes, a feeling of rejection is just that – a false emotion.

Rejection can be very real, however, such as the realization that you were the last one chosen for a sports team or you were overlooked for a job promotion. What about the rejection a person feels when a boyfriend, girlfriend or even a spouse leaves you to be with someone else?

Some people tend to suffer rejection more than others. It could be because of the way they look or even act. No one really wants to be around a sarcastic person or a "know it all" individual. Few of us have ever been rejected by our parents but there are some people who have. This can be the most serious type of rejection – having our own parents reject us. When a person studies the life of Lee Harvey Oswald, (the man accused of killing John F. Kennedy) it will become obvious that even from the time he was a small boy, he suffered every type of rejection possible. He was abandoned by his father, and later, his mother treated him as if he were worthless. He was ostracized by all of his school mates and looked down upon by his teachers. Years later, when he married the beautiful Russian woman Marion, she treated him so badly by berating him and having numerous affairs. Since no one came into his life to break the cycle of rejection and show him the hope of a better life in Christ, well, you know the rest of the story.

Is there no way to escape being rejected? Well, no, I don't think so. None of us can go through life and be on top all the time.

Rejection can pursue a person from birth to our old age. Since we know there will be those "rejection" experiences in everyone's life, what then shall we do to be prepared for them?

First, if God has adopted you as His child, then you can learn to overcome feeling of rejection. It will only work to the measure that you come to believe and receive the absolute truth that no matter who you are or where you've come from – you are forever "accepted in the Beloved" (See Ephesians 1:6). That means God loves you, accepts you unconditionally and will never leave or forsake you. Others may reject or desert you, but God never will.

He is also our guide and our provider. If you get overlooked or rejected by or in anything, it's because He has something far better for you. "But we ought always to thank God for you, brothers loved by the Lord, because from the beginning God chose you to be saved through the sanctifying work of the Spirit and through belief in the truth" (2 Thess. 2:13, NIV).

"Dear friends, do not be surprised at the painful trial you are suffering, as though something strange were happening to you. But rejoice that you participate in the sufferings of Christ, so that you may be overjoyed when his glory is revealed" (1 Peter 4:12, NIV).

"Dear friends, now we are children of God, and what we will be has not yet been made known. But we know that when He appears, we shall be like Him, for we shall see Him as He is" (1 John 3: 2-3, NIV).

What is True Repentance?

Being sorry for what you have done is not necessarily repentance. Genuine repentance is more than "sorry you got caught" or "sorry you have to reap the consequences for that sin." In God's eyes, repentance means "stopping your bad behavior" and turning from those wrong actions. It is simply agreeing with God that what you have done is sin and then asking Him for strength not to continue with the wrong doing.

When I was in the third grade, I tried to cheat on my spelling test because I had forgotten to study. My teacher spotted me. Then I felt not only embarrassment and shame but also fear that my Daddy would find out. Years later, I was offered a copy of my eleventh grade geometry final exam that our teacher's son had stolen from his office. Even though I wanted a good grade, I was not even tempted to cheat because, by then, I had given my heart to the Lord. You see, God has always been merciful to me. In the third grade incident, my Dad never discovered I had done anything wrong, and then, in the eleventh grade, I was able to make a good solid B without cheating.

In the book of Genesis, Esau's younger brother Jacob had not only taken his birthright but had later deceitfully received Esau's blessing from their father, Issac. Even though Jacob had wronged his older brother, God evidently allowed it because Esau didn't really care about the things of God. Later, it appears that he waned to change but according to the Bible, "Esau never found a place of repentance even though he sought it with tears." Sin is more than just doing wrong . Not accepting God's salvation as offered by His son, Jesus Christ, is the basis of all sin.

The Psalmist reflects the despair of someone in sin. "My guilt has overwhelmed me like a burden too heavy to bear" (Psalm 38:4, NIV). Later the Psalmist describes the beginning of repentance. "I confess my iniquity; I am troubled by my sin" (Psalm 38:4, NIV). The apostle John explains the duty of every Christian. "If we confess our sins, he is faithful and just and will forgive our sins and purify us from all unrighteousness" (1 John 1:9).

When that last stage is honestly performed with one's whole heart, then true repentance occurs. Don't be like self-serving Esau and never be able to come to full repentance or there will no doubt come a time in your life that it will be too late to be able to fully repent and then be able to receive God's forgiveness.

Time is God's Gift to Us

Busy, busy people. We all are. Working or retired, our time simply slips away. And then, it is gone forever. It is very important that we try to make the best possible use of our time before it is too late. We must learn to redeem our time, for it is God's precious gift to us.

The other day, I overheard my friend Doug Valeska say to a young female police officer, "There are only 24 hours in a day, I need 42!" I couldn't agree with him more. It seems like every day there is more and more to do. Our lives are so busy that we often put off important things by promising ourselves that we will get to them later at a more convenient time. Unfortunately in most cases, that time never comes.

I have learned, however, if we are faithful to do those things that God prompts us to do, then He will make time for us to get all of our other work done. The wisdom from God is found In Ephesians 5:15,16: "Be very careful, then, how you live-not as unwise, but as wise, making the most of every opportunity because the days are evil" (Ephesians 5:15-16, NIV).

There have been many times, that I have been awakened in the middle of the night with someone's name or face in my thoughts. At first, I wanted to go back to sleep and chose not to listen to those little prompts. Now, however, I know that God is encouraging me to pray for that individual, so I am obedient. On this earth, I may never know how God may be working in that person's life. All I need to know is that He woke me up to pray, so I will obey. Often, I will sit down with a good book or tune in on a special television show that I have been waiting to watch, when the phone rings and there is someone on the line who needs a word of encouragement or simply someone to listen.

We all have opportunities like that. Are we irritated? Or, do we remember just how many times we have called someone to talk to us or to pray with us about a matter.

Last Sunday, our pastor Van Gaute' urged us to always be willing to share the "hope that we had within us" and to always be prepared to tell others about the Good News of Jesus Christ. Are we always willing to do just that? God's word reminds us to "Be wise in the way you act toward outsiders, make the most of every opportunity"(Colossians 4:5, NIV).

Have you ever felt impressed to write a letter or visit a friend or spend time with your parents? In Psalm 89:47 we are instructed to "remember how fleeting is my life." You may never have tomorrow. Take time today. Do whatever your heavenly Father has laid on your heart to do, and then someday, that song, "Thank you, Lord, for sending them to me," will all be about you. More importantly, you will hear, "Well done, good and faithful servant! You have been faithful with a few things; I will put you in charge of many things" (Matthew 25:21, NIV).

The Blessings of a Righteous Inheritance

Many people have been greatly blessed because of the righteous lives of their parents and grandparents before them. I am so thankful for the godly parents that I had. This certainly doesn't mean that they were perfect, but simply that in the eyes of God, He saw them like He saw His son Jesus. That is the true reward for those who have put their hope and faith in our Loving heavenly Father. The Bible mentions many times that one of the rewards of those who live according to God's will is to secure the blessings of God upon their offspring. "The righteous man leads a blameless life; blessed are his children after him" (Proverbs 20:7, NIV). In another passage we are reminded that God punishes the children for the sins of the fathers to the third and fourth generations but He shows love to "a thousand generations of those who love me and keep my commandments" (Exodus 20:5-6, NIV).

It is always rewarding to follow the lives of families such as the Maddox family, the children and grandchildren of Dr. Sam and Mrs. Nadine Maddox. Not only are all three of their sons walking according to God's will but also their wives and their children. It is a real encouragement to see this godly line continue.

But what about those who don't come from Christian homes? There is a second plan. A former governor of Tennessee named Ben Hooper has blessed the lives of so many when he shared his story of being born to an unwed mother. He was drawn to church early in life but always feared anyone asking him who his Daddy was. One day, the pastor of the church managed to catch young Ben before He left services and asked that very question.

Seeing the young boy's face and sensing his embarrassment, the preacher said out loud, "Oh, I know whose child you are. You look just like your father." The child was taken by surprise until he suddenly realized that because he had recently become a Christian, this kindly man was simply commenting on Ben's Heavenly Father who had now claimed him as His very own. That young boy never forgot that encouragement, and often shared that story long after he had become governor of Tennessee.

The much loved pastor of Calvary Baptist church has a very similar story to share. When he was young, he had been placed in foster homes until his mother married Mr. Van Gaute. All of his longing to have a real father and to be loved became a reality when he was adopted and even given the same name as his adopted father. More importantly, Pastor Van soon received Jesus as his Savior and Lord so now there is no doubt who his real father is.

This beautiful song says it all: "I have a Father. He knows my Name. He knows my every thought. He sees each tear that falls, and hears me when I call."

If you don't have a righteous inheritance through your biological bloodline, you can have one when you receive the King of King and the Lord of Lords as your Savior. When the Lord God is your Father, His blessings are permanent.

What Does the Bible Say About Death?

"Do not be deceived: God cannot be mocked. A man reaps what he sows. The one who sows to please his sinful nature, from that nature will reap destruction; the one who sows to please the Spirit; from the Spirit will reap eternal life" (Galatians 6:7-8, NIV).

It has been said, and many times over, that no one leaves this world alive, and that is true, except for maybe Enoch, who so walked with God that the Father took him. Well, there is also Elijah who went up in a chariot of fire. But, it is quite evident that death must come to us all.

How then does one prepare to die? Older people feel its pressure, but the young rarely do. In fact, having to die is usually the fartherest thing from their minds; yet, at an alarming rate, more and more young people are dying due to accidents – especially car wrecks, overdose of drugs, disease and even war. Strangely, death often creeps up on a person who is obviously not ready to go.

There was a young man who faced testicular cancer. He knew there was the imminent possibility that he would die. Only in his early twenties, the courageous young man said, "I've been raised in a Christian home and I came to the Lord at a young age. I knew where I'd be going, but I didn't feel that I had finished what God had for me to do, so I fought the cancer hard." Thankfully, God healed him and he didn't have to face death this time.

What about all the many young people who are taken on from this world without healing being given on this side? There again, death comes for them. When it is our time, then all of us will die. A.B. Simpson, noted theologian, has said, "No one will exit this planet until their mission in life is complete."

Some, however, start out of this world only to have God send them back for a longer life. Such was the case of Barbara Williams. In March of 1978, Mrs. Williams went into the hospital for routine surgery. She had an adverse reaction to either the anesthesia or the pain medication and coded on the table. All she could hear was, "Her blood pressure has bottomed out. I can't find a pulse."

Barbara distinctly remembers being in a great deal of pain when suddenly the pain started leaving as she felt herself drifting out of her body and begin traveling toward a brilliant white light at the end of the tunnel she was somehow passing through. "Words can't describe the pure white light I saw. I felt peace, love and contentment. There was the most awesome music," she explained.

About this time physicians and medical personnel were working on her body, and she had to return to it even though she says "I didn't want to come back."

Before this happened to her, Barbara related that she had always believed that she had been born into the wrong family since she did not have the talents that other members of her family enjoyed. However, almost at once after her "near death" experience, Barbara began to do creative things like writing poems, magazine articles and even dramas. Is it possible that creativity goes along with being near the Creator?

Therefore, even though just as we are now living, we are all one day destined to die. Death should never be feared by a child of God for the Bible makes it very clear that "Precious in the sight of the Lord is the death of his saints" (Psalm 116:25, NIV). The Bible also explains that "death is the destiny of every man" (Ecclesiastes 7:2, NIV). Nevertheless, the Bible assures us that one day Our Lord God "will swallow up death forever" (Isaiah 25: 8, NIV).

My Father's Christmas Gift

Shortly after Daddy was born, his own father wrote a prayer in the form of a poem for his newborn son. It was filled with all the wishes and hopes for this child's future. A godly father wrote down his deepest desires for his son's life. Little did Joseph Pinckney Jones know at the time that he would never live to see the little fellow grow up. Evidently, Joe Jones wrote his prayer, shut his accounting book where he wrote it and tucked it inside his desk drawer. My own father never knew anything about this poem since Joe Jones died when my Dad was only four.

Even though my grandmother did everything she could to bring up her two sons to be good Christian boys, both of them longed to have a father. My daddy often talked about how safe he felt when he spent the night in the homes of his friends who had fathers. Since he had desperately wanted a father, he tried to be the very best daddy to his four daughters that he could possibly be.

Because we all loved our father so very much, we always tried to think up things that would please him, especially at Christmas. He had often told us never to buy him anything because if he wanted something, he would buy it himself. The quest to find the perfect gift was always a difficult one every year.

One week-end when I was visiting my grandmother, I decided to look in her old corn crib outside. Inside, I found a lot of boxes and one rustic trunk. As I opened the lid to the trunk, all I saw was pieces of material and an old ledger book. I almost didn't bother to look inside, but I'm so thankful that I did. As I thumbed through the pages, I saw only columns of numbers uniformly written. Getting bored, I almost shut the book until I spotted, in very stilted handwriting, "Little J. P. Jones." As I read the poem, tears sprang to my eyes. I realized that I had found a treasure. It was written by my grandfather about my father. It was dated May 24, 1914 and signed Mr. And Mrs. J. P. Jones.

My mother and I took the original poem and had it sealed and framed. Then we all had to wait until Christmas to see what Daddy would say. I'll never forget that Christmas morning as our family sat around the tinseled laden tree. For once, none of us were thinking about what we would be getting, but only about our father's Christmas present. When Mother pulled the present out from under our tree and handed it to Daddy, he frowned at first as he perhaps wondered what the odd shaped gift would be. He read the tag; "With love to Daddy from all of us." As he tore the package open, he scrunched up his face and then there was silence. Tears were nestling in his eyes as he willed himself not to cry. I broke the silence by announcing how I had found the poem outside in Mama Annie's old corn crib. By then, we were all crying except for our dad who was making every effort not to.

Daddy had never really been able to know much about his earthly father, but he could now have no doubt how much his dad had loved him. That poem in the form of a prayer had actually come to pass. Joseph Paul had become the man his father had prayed he would become all those years ago. From the grave, his father's words filled an immense void in his life.

Today, as all of us Jones girls celebrate the Christmas season, we still remember that one special Christmas when our father received the best Christmas gift of his life. Both our parents are now in Heaven with those who have gone before us. Because of the Christ child, we all have hope of seeing them all again.

"Take delight in the Lord, and He will give you your heart's desires;" (Psalm 37:4, NLT).

What Does God Require of a Man?

A number of years ago, I heard former District Attorney, Tom Sorrells, do a humorous sketch at a banquet. In closing, he got more serious and shared a wonderful short speech on what was really important in life – one's true character. He quoted from the Old Testament prophet Micah. 6:8: "He has showed you, O Man, what is good and what does the Lord require of you? To act justly and to love mercy and to walk humbly with your God" (Micah 6:8, NIV). That speech certainly made an impact on me.

In thinking about all that Tom said that night, I was reminded of two significant events that happened which directly concerned my father, J. P. Jones. I was a teenager when the first story was used to impact the second one.

My Dad lost his own father when he was only four years old, and his younger brother, Lamar, was just two. My grandmother never remarried, but she did her best to bring up her two boys to become men of integrity.

Once my father got angry with a teacher and quit school. My grandmother reminded him that "pride goes before a fall." She also reminded him that he would never amount to anything without an education. When at last he repented, he went to school and apologized.

In order to be allowed to return to class he was required to transport a huge pile of dirt from a dump site to his high school where they were building a new classroom. He swallowed his pride, took the dirt in a wheelbarrow load by load until he finally completed his task. His friends and classmates stood on the sidelines cheering on my handsome Dad who was walking, shirtless and smiling as he pushed the dirt all the way to the school. It actually worked out for the best and added to his popularity.

Years later, a friend of mine, Charlie Monk, sassed our English teacher, Ms. Annette Redmon, and she not only kicked him out of class; she wouldn't allow him to keep his part in our senior play that she was directing. He was to play the part of my father in the comedy "Turn Back the Clock". The role went to his best friend, Joe Frank Kilpatrick.

Heartbroken, Charlie Monk quit school and went to live in downtown Geneva Hotel. That's where my father took me to talk to my friend. "You're made out of good stuff, Charlie, and you'll never amount to anything without a good education. Now you just swallow your pride and get back to school or I'll whip your rear end." Of course, he also told Charlie about his own episode of quitting school and of the consequences he had to pay in order to return. Thankfully, Charlie Monk listened to my father, finished school, and ultimately, has become a big name in the music industry in Nashville, Tennessee.

All of us make mistakes, and sometimes, the consequences of those wrong choices can ruin our lives. On the other hand, God always gives us a way out if we'll let him. He freely offers us chance after chance until we get it right. We each have a free will, and we can even now repent of our wrong doings and ask for another chance. God is there just waiting for us to ask Him to help us.

- "He guides the humble in what is right and teaches them his way" (Psalm 25:9, NIV).
- "He mocks proud mockers and gives grace to the humble" (Proverbs 3:34, NIV).
- James 4:10 "Humble yourselves before the Lord, and he will lift you up" (James 4:10, NIV).

- "The fear of the LORD teaches a man wisdom , and humility comes before honor" (Proverbs 15:33, NIV).

God's Appointed Times

It has been said that it is important to be in the right place at the right time. That was certainly true of former Auburn football player, Ronnie Ross. As captain of his team in 1970, Ronnie excelled at his position at tight end. However, Ross is best known for his performance one day when he was sent in to play linebacker. All of the starters were injured and "Shug" Jordan sent Ronnie in to take that slot. At that time, Alabama was leading 17 to 7 and the Tide was on its way to make another touchdown. At Auburn's 10 yard line, Ross intercepted a pass by Alabama's star quarterback, Scott Hunter. The Tiger fans went wild. That one play evidently gave the War Eagle team just the spark they needed because they went on to win the game 33 to 28.

Later, when asked how he felt about his thrilling interception, Ross commented to a sportswriter, "I had no clue what I was doing or where I was supposed to be." Obviously, for Auburn anyway, he was just in the right place at the right time. Everyone spoke highly of Ronnie Ross. He even had many friends on Alabama's team. It was said of Ronnie that if anyone had a problem, he would be right there to try to help them. Most all of his friends had a pair of "Ronnie Ross" sunglasses because that's what he sold after graduation. He also acted as a promoter for his brother, boxer "Mad Dog" Ross. For some reason, the very handsome and talented Ronnie never reached his full potential. In fact, he never even got married.

One day, as Ronnie lay in a Pensacola hospital dying of lung cancer, two of his close friends, Mike "Captain Crunch" Kolen, who played for Auburn and Steve Baumhauer, a former Crimson Tide starter, visited him. Since both men were very strong Christians, they wanted to make sure Ronnie got right with the Good Lord. Again, Ross was at the right place at the right time. He recognized his need to be saved and prayed that day to receive Christ. That was his appointed time. Later, in his weakened condition, Ross led another friend of his to the Lord.

Ronnie Ross died December 8, 2009. Lee Gross, also a former Tiger player and father of baseball great, Gabe Gross, told our Life Connection Group at Calvary Baptist about his funeral. "People were crying one minute, and laughing the next" he said. There were guys from all over the state, Alabama and Auburn alike. Mike Kolen preached his funeral service.

Ronnie Ross was a good man but he could have never made it into heaven no matter how great his football playing was or how much he did for others without having received Christ. "For with the heart one believes to righteousness, and with the mouth confession is made to salvation. For the Scripture says, 'Whoever believes on Him will not be put to shame'" (Romans 10:10-11, NIV).

Gossip is Becoming a National Pastime

From the tabloid magazines to the back of a church's choir room, secrets that are suddenly not secrets at all are broadcast freely. The yen to know everything that is going on with other people is an inborn natural desire. We are all creatures of curiosity. But, why then, would God command that we, as Christians, not gossip? If it is an inner trait of us all, then how can we not succumb to it?

God knows our natural bent. He also promises to give us strength to overcome anything that will not profit us personally. He will also strengthen us so we will bring harm to someone else.

It is bad enough to spread tales when the news is true, but even more tragic when the information is totally false. Case in point, a young girl named Annie was being sexually abused by her own father. Since a neighbor man found the little girl crying one day, he gently picked her up to console her. Someone saw him and when Annie became pregnant by her own father, that person told everyone that this neighbor was responsible. Even though he was totally innocent, the vicious rumor caused him to be labeled a "child molester." He lost his family because his wife believed what was told about him. What actually happened was the same thing as his being murdered. For our character is dear and precious to us, and his good name was forever ruined because little Annie did not have the courage to tell the truth. She was so afraid of her father.

There are also many instances where people misjudge what they actually see with their own eyes. Once, when a prominent man passed out from a problem with his heart, it was told he had been drunk because it happened near a liquor store. Instead of someone covering his apparent problem with love, it was gleefully reported to the detriment of everyone concerned.

We've all heard the story about someone dumping a sack full of feathers from the top of a tall building. Try as one might, all those feathers could never be adequately recovered. That's what happens when gossip is repeated over and over. True or not, the story that is told is believed.

There is also the old adage "where there is smoke, there is fire." Meaning of course, if there is a suspicion, there must be some truth to it.

Actually, whether what we repeat is true or not is not the problem. The real truth is that no matter what, we should not be guilty of saying or doing anything that could bring further harm to someone. If a person is guilty, eventually, "all hidden things will be brought to light," and it is not up to us to help make that happen. "But there is a God in heaven who reveals secrets" (Daniel 2:27, NLT). God is in control. If the story is untrue, we will not be guilty of falsely accusing someone.

What can we do if we are being told some juicy gossip? Try to change the subject, and above all, don't repeat it. Gossip is one sin that affects everyone. Unfortunately many Christians do not notice or believe that it is sinful. God has a different viewpoint. His word reveals that we are never to be guilty of harming – in any way – another person.

- "Whenever we have the opportunity, we should do good to everyone" (Galatians 6: 10, NLT).
- "God blesses those who are merciful, for they will be shown mercy" (Matthew 5:7, NLT).
- "I will watch my ways and keep my tongue from sin, I will put a muzzle on my mouth" (Psalm 39:1, NIV).

- "If anyone considers himself religious and yet does not keep a tight rein on his tongue, he deceives himself and his religion is worthless" (James 1:26, NIV).
- "But no man can tame the tongue, it is a restless evil, full of deadly poison" (James 3:8, NIV).

One of my New Year's resolutions is not to be guilty of gossiping. I pray I can avoid this sin and never spread true or, certainly, untrue stories about someone else unless it is good and positive news. Don't let the world squeeze you into its mold!

Help When Life Serves you Disappointment

Every person has suffered a disappointment in their lifetime, probably more than a few times. Being disappointed can only result in having an expected end somehow not happening in the way you believed it would be. We can be disappointed in a job, a marriage, our children, etc. Disappointments come over spoiled events, lost opportunities and even plans that don't come to fruition.

All human beings can understand what disappointment is. We know how it hurts and how long that feeling usually lingers. From early childhood to our old age, disappointment wedges itself into our lives and brings with it as much discomfort as possible.

Where is the relief from this vicious draining emotion? Is there help? Well, I firmly believe there is. First of all, it is a fact that God is never disappointed. He can't experience disappointment because He knows the end from the beginning. He has no false expectations because He knows what every outcome will be. If you are a Christian you should be comforted by these Scriptures. "I know, O Lord, that a man's life is not his own; it is not for man to direct his steps" (Jeremiah 10:23, NIV). Job also understood that no plan of God's could be thwarted (Job 42:2, NIV). God's promise to us is secure. – Jeremiah 29:11 "For I know the plans I have for you declares the Lord, plans to prosper you and not to harm you, plans to give you a hope and a future" (Jeremiah 29:11, NIV).

In an interview with Christian author and former atheist, Josh McDowell, he shared with me his greatest disappointment which ultimately resulted in his biggest blessing. When his girlfriend broke up with him, his heart was broken. Watching her wave goodbye to him as he was flying out of town, Josh said God spoke to him, "Don't you trust me to give you something better?" He couldn't imagine anything better than the woman he had just lost, until he met the young lady who later became his wife and the mother of his children. "Wow", he exclaimed, "Is God ever great! If I had married that other girl, just think what I would have missed!"

I could also cite incident after incident in my own life where a "disappointment" resulted in a wonderful outcome for me.

So, the next time you feel let down or disappointed, pause, take a deep breath and give this situation to the Lord. I even thank Him for taking my "seeming" roadblock and turning it into a miracle for me. Try it and then let me know the result. I dare you!

What has Been cut off From Your Life?

As long as we are in this world, all of us must face change. Some are good and some not so good. Sometimes change is devastating. For example, the loss of something very precious to us may devastate us. It could be a loved one through death or divorce. Perhaps it might be a job or position we held dear. It often is our health or sometimes, parts of our very own bodies. Change happened to the world renowned Golden Knight, Dana Bowman, when his own legs were literally amputated from his body in mid-air by his sky-diving partner. Just try to imagine the shock and horror of watching someone's arms hit against your legs so forcefully that they caused your limbs to be totally severed right in front of your eyes. To add to Bowman's loss, his close friend died moments later due to the impact. One sorrow followed after another when later, Bowman's new bride left him.

Miraculously, Dana Bowman survived everything that has happened to him. Today, he is a role model for others who have faced similar situations. His life was blessed recently when he discovered a new product designed and manufactured right here in Dothan to help his prosthetic device function much more comfortably. This revolutionary liner system was designed and produced by Prosthetist Rick Scussell and Orthopedic Surgeon David Alford from Southern Bone and Joint. This marvelous Symmetry Liner system has so improved Bowman's life that he can wear his prosthetic device all day long without having to loosen or change it. "It's amazing" Bowman exclaims!

Pretty amazing, too, is Dana Bowman's life today. Nothing seems to stop him, no matter if he doesn't have his original legs. Observing closely his life, one can only surmise that if Bowman can get back up, so can we. Just like one of my all time heroes, World War II flying ace Douglas Bader who also had to have his legs amputated following a plane crash, Bowman chose to live on and become constructive not just wallow around in self-pity. Bader strapped on those original prosthetic legs and took a pretty girl dancing even as his stumps were bleeding and he suffered great pain. Wouldn't he have rejoiced to see what is possible today with the new liner system?

All of us face these kinds of "amputations" in life when things, as we have always known them, come to a radical halt. With Our Lord's loving guidance we can become aware of an even bigger sphere in which to continue in this life. Please don't grieve continually over what has been cut off from your present life; choose to trust Him to give you something else. Most of the time when God gives something else it is ten times better than what you have lost. Remember these comforting verses: "God is our refuge and strength, an ever-present help in trouble. Therefore we will not fear, though the earth give way and the mountains fall into the heart of the sea" (Psalm 46:1-2, NIV). If we really understand God's character and His power, we can surrender all to his will and be at peace. As someone wrote once, "All sunshine makes a desert." When the rains of pain come tumbling down, we can rest assured that "There is a river whose streams make glad the city of God" (Psalm 46:4, NIV).

God's Eye is on the Sparrow

One of my favorite songs is "His Eye is On the Sparrow." In fact, it was one of the very first songs that I sang at church when I was around eleven years old. That song has impacted my life in so many ways. The Word of God tells us that God's eye is on the sparrow. In Luke 12: 6 and 7 it says, "Are not five sparrows sold for two pennies? Yet not one of them is forgotten by God. Indeed, the very hairs of your head are all numbered. Don't be afraid, you are worth more than many sparrows" (Luke 12:6-7, NIV). To me, Jesus is saying that if God provides for the little sparrow, how much more will he take care of His children?

That verse was brought back to me when my husband and I got the chance to meet a darling little two year old Native American girl named "Nae nae" We had just arrived at the Amtrack station in Chicago in preparation for our Great California Train trip when we became enthralled with this tiny little miss. Almost immediately she spotted Jerome sitting there smiling at her. For some reason all children love Jerome. Nae nae climbed right up into his lap and proceeded to have him "read" to her in a magazine. She was so smart that she always remembered what he had told her about each thing on the page. Once he started talking to another member of our travelers and she immediately turned his face back toward her saying, "Daddy, read me the book." He obeyed, of course.

While this was going on, I moved over to the lady who was traveling with the precocious two year old and asked if she were the mother. "Now, I am" said the African American woman. "I have just signed the final adoption papers today and we are now on our way home."

Always the interviewer, I had to ask the woman all about how she got Nae nae. Actually, it was a story that proved more than ever God's watch care over us all. Minnie confessed that she had always wanted a baby of her own but was unable to have children. One day, Minnie had flown to another state to visit a friend of hers and was sitting out on her friend's porch, when a beautiful young woman who was obviously in pain, started by the residence. Spotting Minnie, the woman came over to where she sat and said, "would you please take me to the emergency room? I am in labor and am about to have a baby." Quickly, Minnie grabbed her friend's car keys and took the pregnant lady to the hospital. Even though the mother did not look pregnant, she delivered a tiny infant girl who weighed just a few pounds and could easily fit in the palm of one's hand.

As soon as the little one was delivered, her mother got up and dismissed herself telling the woman at the desk that she wanted Minnie to have her baby. It was touch and go for many days, but finally, little Nae nae made it with surrogate mom Minnie by her side the entire time. It was quite awhile before the adoption could be made legal but from day one, Minnie knew she wanted this precious child. In God's providence, He causes everything to fit or come together at the right time. Minnie got her child and Nae nae found someone to love her. An accident? You decide. God always provides for those of us who belong to Him.

"My God shall supply all your need according to His riches in glory by Christ Jesus" (Philippians 4:19, NIV).

Lord, Help us to Stand

Each one of us may face situations in life that continue to baffle us. We pray and wait, but no answer seems to come. The Psalmist admonishes us to "Rest in the lord, and wait patiently for him to act" (Psalm 37:7, NIV). However, in our humanity, we find it difficult to wait when we desire something so strongly. In our dilemma, we have a choice, we can either believe what God has promised us, or we can give up before the victory is won. Whenever God gives us His word on a matter, it is already accomplished in His mind. God is not capricious. God speaks to us through the prophet Isaiah; "What I have said, that will I bring about; what I have planned, that will I do" (Isaiah 46:11, NIV).

If we are assured that we genuinely have a promise from the Lord, then our place is to stand on His word continuously until we actually see it come to pass. In the footnotes to Daniel 8:18 (which tells how God's spirit moved on Daniel "he touched me and made me stand upright") states "Make me stand upon my standing." It is God's strengthening power that causes us to stand, to have faith and trust in His word to us. We ought to remember that without faith it is impossible to please Him. (See Hebrews 11:6, NIV).

Jack Taylor tells the story of a woman who had been deserted by her husband while she was carrying their son. In deep despair, she had fallen on her knees begging God to show her what to do. In her heart, she felt that He promised her that her child would one day preach the Gospel. He also assured her that He would meet every need that she had.

Years went by, and the mother had done her best to bring her son up in the Christian faith; however, that young boy had been sent to prison because he was hanging out with the wrong crowd. One day, she received a telegram from the warden of the prison stating that her son had been killed in a prison riot. The grieving mother fell to her knees in shock and unbelief. Then, as she cried, something moved in her heart. In desperation, she ran to get her Bible where she had marked all the promises God had given her about her son. She lifted up that open Bible with one hand and the telegram from the warden in the other. "God, she pleaded, either your word is true or this telegram is. I choose to believe your Word that my son is alive so that he can preach the Gospel." Soon the telephone rang and the warden at the prison called to apologize. It was not her son that had died but another inmate. Her son was recuperating in the prison infirmary. Today, that same boy (now a man) is preaching the Gospel. That's the kind of faith I'm talking about.

Maltbie D. Babcock wrote many years ago: "Pay as little attention to discouragement as possible, plough ahead as a steamer does, rough or smooth, rain or shine." God's promises are always "yes, and amen." Nothing can ultimately prevent His Word to you from coming true. We have to have patience and wait on His timing. Lord, help us to stand and then to "stand on our standing."

What is the Measure of a Man?

"He has showed you, O Man, what is good. And what does the lord require of you? To act justly and to love mercy and to walk humbly with your God" (Micah 6:8, NIV).

The first time I saw him, he was wearing a wrinkled blue swim trunk, topped with a short-sleeved white shirt. His chest hairs shone proudly under his open shirt and on his head, he sported a very worn old fishing hat. Lovely blue eyes crinkled as he said while waving his fishing reel in his hand," I'm ready to go fishing!" He was not at all what I had expected. In my mind, he didn't look like the well trained professional I had imagined. I was soon to learn that my new friend was never exactly what you could define in normal terms.

Years later, I rushed into his office with red spots all over me. "It's not the measles," he said. And, because he was who he was, I believed him and went home in peace. I was expecting my first child and had been afraid that while teaching school, I had been exposed to the German measles that were going around which could be very dangerous for my baby.

It has been my pleasure through the years to know this man both professionally and personally. He was a remarkable man. Never fitting into any box or wearing any sort of label, he was a genuine original. And, though he will be greatly missed, his legacy lives on. It lives on in his wife, Jane, of over 57 years, and in his children and grandchildren. They have a marvelous inheritance. For no matter what Dr. Buren Wells accomplished in the way of earthly goals, what he managed to do in the area of what really counts in today's world is rare indeed. First, he unashamedly accepted the Lord Jesus as his Savior and Lord. He loved his church and faithfully attended. His three children were secure that their father honestly loved their mother because he said so over and over, marveling as how marrying her was the best thing that he had ever done. He not only said he loved all his offspring, but he showed it by spending quality time with them on world class "Wells' Family vacations".

Buren Wells was a man of integrity and knew the value of hard work. He also taught his family never to give up. Once, after sewing up his daughter's leg following an accident, he encouraged her to go on and swim in the swimming tournament. Buren was tough but compassionate. Remarkably, not only did his son speak about his Dad at the funeral but also his son-in-law. Their equal love and admiration was apparent.

Today, Buren is enjoying his eternal rewards. I believe he is singing in the heavenly choir. He told us one time how he had always wanted to sing in the college choir. Because he kept going to try-outs each time, the leader had pity on him and finally said "Buren, you can be in the choir, but don't sing! You just mouth the words." So, that's exactly what he did. Today Buren Wells is a star singer up there! By whatever measure one has as to what denotes greatness, this man passed the test. Let us strive to do likewise.

Selective Memory

Recently, I listened as a young woman extolled the virtues of her recently deceased ex-boyfriend. They had broken up over a year before he died, but all of a sudden, she was only able to remember his virtues and none of his faults. This unreal remembrance of her old beau was damaging her present relationship with the new man in her life.

"Don't you remember why you broke up with him?" a friend questioned. "Even though he had a charming personality," she continued, "You left him because he physically abused you, and he would never get a job! Why can't you see this?" she finished.

I don't think anyone can change the person who is stuck with "selective memory." It must be a quirk in human nature to reminisce on only the good, or conversely, some people choose to remember just the bad memories and experiences and none of the truly pleasant ones. Why is this?

I believe it is simply a choice or frame of mind. Years ago, I was trying to counsel someone who was going through a difficult time in her marriage. She decided to get a divorce. As I attempted to try to encourage her to consider reconciliation, she began unfolding a note from inside her purse. On it she had written a list of her spouse's faults. The trembling woman then began to read it out loud. Her thoughts were solidly set to think of nothing else but the bad experiences in her marriage and none of the positive ones.

I confess I have been guilty of doing both – choosing to think of only an idealistic picture of past relationships or on the other hand, becoming embittered as I recalled things that had been done or said to me. I do have a tendency to idealize people

I love dearly – like my grandmother who died when I was only twenty years old.

As I have grown as a Christian, however, I have learned how to almost always overcome "selective memory" and that is to choose to "have the mind of Christ" in every situation I face in life.

> When we receive Christ, we are freely given this promise in the word of God: "But we have the mind of Christ" (1 Corinthians 2:16, NIV).

> With the Holy Spirit within us, we can adhere to Paul's admonition. "Do not conform any longer to the pattern of this world, but be transformed by the renewing of your mind" (Romans 12:2, NIV).

> The Bible promises that we can "be made new in the attitude of your minds" (Ephesians 4:23, NIV).

> And, finally, "Your attitude should be the same as that of Christ Jesus" (Philippians, 2:5, NIV).

With all of that being absolutely true, we don't have to deal with the problems of "selective memory". Instead, we can think and even remember our past with clear, unbiased thoughts. We can reflect without judgment, bitterness or even unrealistic idealization. Because we have been given the "mind of Christ," we can think clearly as He empowers us to do so, knowing that all that has happened before truly works for our good and His glory. (See Romans 8:28).

How to Spot a Winner

Katie was only four, but she already knew she was a winner. Perkily, she pranced into her first day at gymnastics—all smiles. After class, her entire attitude changed. "Where's my trophy?" the child demanded. "I want my trophy!" Quickly, her mother explained that no one ever got a prize the first day. However, she said, "If you work very hard, one day you will win one." Immediately, little Katie threw her arms into the air like in the "Rocky" movie as she headed to the car yelling "I'm a winner! I'm a winner!" She believed it in her heart and that's what's important.

Adults can learn a lot from children. A few weeks ago, our pastor's grandson was out in the yard swinging with his father, Kurt, when the three year old began talking about "perseverance." "Zack," his amazed father asked, "do you even know what that word means?" "Yes, the little boy spouted. "It means 'Never give up!'" Zack, too, got it!

One way the Weight Watcher's organization helps their clients lose weight is by changing their perception of themselves, explains my daughter-in-law, Karen. While teaching her class recently she urged the members to quit saying, "I've always been fat and I'll always be fat!" Instead, overweight folks should be like the "Little Train That Could." In the story, the small train kept saying "I think I can, I think I can, I think I can" etc until it was over the top of the hill. In the case of weight loss strugglers over the battle of the bulge victory comes.

So many examples are found in the Bible of winners. Joseph believed God's promise even when he was sold into slavery by his brothers, and later, wrongfully imprisoned. The rest of the story tells how in one day Joseph saw God's word come to pass when he was elevated to the throne of all Egypt to be second in command next to Pharaoh. Moses left the luxuries of Egypt to align himself with his biological Hebrew family. He hid in the desert until God called him to deliver His people from slavery. The Apostle Paul was an ultimate winner when he made the decision to follow Christ and to become leader of the very people he had once persecuted.

Every person may be a winner in life. It does not matter what the odds are or what circumstances look like. If we truly belong to Jesus, we can see ourselves as an overcomer. With perseverance, it is possible to keep our eyes on the goal He has set before us, and then we can learn to trust Him to bring us through until the end of all time. It is our God who determines that we should be winners! Let the Bible be the source of your encouragement.

- "I press on toward the goal to win the prize for which God has called me heavenward in Christ Jesus" (Philippians 3:14, NIV).
- "I can do everything through him who gives me strength" (Philippians 4:13, NIV).
- "I pray that out of his glorious riches he may strengthen you with power through his Spirit in your inner being" (Ephesians 3:16, NIV).
- "Now to him who is able to do immeasurably more than all we ask or imagine, according to his power that is at work within us" (Ephesians 3:20, NIV).

God's Ways are Often Hard to Understand

Even for the person who has walked with the Lord for many years, God's ways are not easy to discern. In Scripture, it is written, "For my thoughts are not your thoughts, neither are your ways my ways,' declares the Lord. 'For as the Heavens are higher than the Earth, so are my ways higher than your ways, and my thoughts than your thoughts'" (Isaiah 55:8-9, NIV). Because we are finite creatures, there are some things that we have to simply accept by faith.

Once a man was questioning why it had been necessary for God to send Jesus as a man to earth so that we could come to know God through his Son. It seemed unreal to this man, and he was not so sure he would ever go along with what others believed in. One day, however, there was a terrible snowstorm where he lived and as he looked out of his window, he saw flocks of birds being plummeted to death by the heavy falling snow.

Immediately, he rushed out to try to save their lives by opening the doors to his barn. But, his efforts were to no avail because he couldn't make the birds understand what he was trying to do. Finally, in desperation, he fell on his knees and cried out, "If only I could become a bird for a time so I could show them the way to save their lives." It was then that he got the message. Jesus had come to earth as a man to do just that. He came to save our souls and to die so that we could have eternal life with Him.

As in the case of the dying birds in the snowstorm, God often uses other creatures to teach us spiritual truths. One such case is the story Roslyn Horton. Her story tells about what she learned from her job as a beekeeper. This is her story.

My bees have taught me a lot about God. One of my most profound experiences happened right before hurricane Ivan came through. I had to prepare my hives for the approaching hurricane to protect them. This is done by putting a cinder block on the hive and then tightening it down. That way if the hive is blown over, at least everything stays together and you don't have bees blown for miles around. The bees knew bad weather was close and were on Red Alert, meaning, they reacted violently to me trying to do what I was doing. I took a lot of stings while trying to help them and by the time I was on the last hive, I was hurting badly. I was also totally frustrated watching bees get wound into the ratchet while I could barely see my hands for them. "YOU STUPID BEES" I thought. There's a storm coming and I'm out here doing everything I can to save your buzzy little rears from getting blown to kingdom come and you're fighting me for all you're worth! The thought had no sooner gone through my head when my heart was pierced. It was like God was saying "Now, you get it!" I could almost hear Him saying, "You stupid humans."

We all can relate to that. When we think God is trying to harm us, in reality, He is there simply trying to help us. So, the next time you are facing a test or a trial in your life, just stop and listen to what God is trying to tell you. If you can't understand, just wait on Him until you do. "As for God, his way is perfect; the word of the Lord is flawless, He is a shield for all who take refuge in him" (Psalm 18:30, NIV).

God's Protection Plan Always Covers Us

Dr. A. B. Simpson said in the early 1900's that no man will ever leave this planet until his mission in life is completed. That could explain why some people escape possible death situations more than once in their lives. Each individual is born with a specific destiny and none so much as a true believer. "All the days ordained for me were written in your book before one of them came to be" (Psalm 139:16, NIV).

A few weeks ago, my husband was having lunch with two of his cousins, James Earl and Leonard Guy. Since neither my husband nor James Earl had seen Leonard in years, they had also never heard the following story. Leonard had been a career military man stationed in Germany. When it came time to fly home, he decided to schedule a trip to England on the way so that his family could see all the historical sites of that country. Four tickets were purchased that would take them to London's Heathrow Airport. After a few days there a direct flight would take them to America. But, there was one problem. His twin daughters had rescued a stray kitten. Even though they had found someone who would take their pet when they left Germany, as the time grew nearer, the two realized they could not bear to leave their cat.

After begging their daddy to allow the family pet to go along, he relented and called the Air Lines to find out how he could carry the cat. To his surprise, Leonard learned the cat would have to be quarantined for six months before being allowed to enter England and if that happened, the poor cat would never be the same. So, the disappointed father asked the man on the phone what he could do. He was told that the family would have to take an entirely different route home bypassing England and also, they would have to pay an extra $125 fee for the cat's flight. Being a loving father, Guy did just that.

And now, for the rest of the story. The very plane the Guy family would have taken home was Pan Am Flight 103 which left Heathrow Airport on Wednesday, December 21, 1988 to fly to New York's John F Kennedy International Airport. Tragically, that was the plane that the Libyan terrorists blew up with a bomb killing all people on board - 243 passengers and 16 crew members. Also, eleven people on the ground in Lockerbie, south Scotland was also killed. After hearing the news that day, Leonard said he pulled out his four tickets scheduled for the "Clipper Maid of the Seas" got down on his knees and praised His Heavenly Father for sparing the life of his entire family including their beloved cat. Leonard still has those tickets today to remind him that God had some reason for allowing all of the Guys to live.

There had been many stories about that flight in the national news media. One other man had arrived late that day and missed the plane, so he was spared also. The story of Sergeant Major Leonard Guy and his family's survival was never told until now in any news source. It certainly shows how much God loved that family to keep them from taking that plane trip on that exact date. Perhaps He was the one who sent the cat. God's Word reminds us of His faithful protection of his children: "See, I have engraved you on the palms of my hands, your walls are ever before me" (Isaiah 49:16, NIV). "The Lord will fulfill his purpose for me" (Psalm 138:8, NIV).

Temptation Highway

A few years ago I did some interviews with prisoners at Bullock County Correctional Facility. The whole purpose of our program was to discover which of these inmates could be rehabilitated. Many of them had been able to change due to programs directed by Chaplain Steve Walker. On the other hand, I also interviewed some who were locked-in because of their willful misbehavior. One such man was a child molester named Terry.

It is difficult to describe how I felt when he sat down beside me, and I looked into his steely blue eyes. At the time, I had no idea what he was in prison for until I asked him. In his presence, I felt pure evil.

As I began the interview, he took on an almost "arrogant attitude" as his story unfolded. Explaining how he tracked down his victims and carefully chose his next "target" to molest seemed to bring him pleasure. I tried my best to not let my feeling show because I'm sure he would have derived enjoyment from that as well.

Later, he began to use terminology that I later became more familiar with and that was "feeding the pig." Anything that excites or leads a predator to more and more temptations such as driving by a playground to watch children is referred to as "feeding the pig." When these sex offenders are released from prison, and they almost always are, they are required to attend regular support groups. The main theme of these gatherings is to teach ex-convicts how not to enter into temptation. They are instructed to totally stay away from children and to avoid child pornography or anything that "feeds the pig."

Well, that is rather graphic, but it simply illustrates a point, and that is, if you are being tempted, flee! Run for your life. The Bible says, "No temptation has seized you except what is common to man. And God is faithful; he will not let you be tempted beyond what you can bear. But when you are tempted, he will provide a way out so that you can stand up under it" (1 Corinthians 10:13, NIV).

If a convicted sex offender can avoid being tempted by following the mandates of a support group of fellow molesters, how much more can we as followers of Christ learn to keep away from our individual temptations?

Your temptation might be over indulgence in food or even addictions to drugs or alcohol. It may be an attraction to someone of the opposite sex who is married. Your temptation might be peanut butter! I know it is one of my greatest "tempting treats". Sometimes, when I am trying so hard to lose weight, that jar of peanut butter calls my name from the cabinet. It is my choice? Ignore it, throw the jar outside in the trash or give in and eat some with a big spoon! It's my decision, and it is yours, too, when you are trying to avoid being tempted.

When I turned fifty, I threw my bathroom scales away. I decided that I would never again be tempted to rule my life by how much I weighed and judging my entire worth on whether I was gaining or losing weight. By the way, my weight has consistently been way down since I did this.

Whatever works for you to overcome falling into temptation, do it! Don't succumb to something that will cause you to pay and pay and pay for what you've done. A friend of mine says she avoids over-eating by quoting, "a moment on my lips but forever on my hips."

If you commit sin, others beside yourself may have to pay for it. Broken homes, broken hearts and broken dreams are killers! Don't give in because you can avoid that pressure; that urging to do those things which God says "Don't do!" or which in the long run will only cause you grief. "Don't feed the pig!" Never wonder down the highway of temptation, because the results may be devastating. "Enter through the narrow gate. For wide is the gate and broad is the road that leads to destruction, and many enter through it. But small is the gate and narrow the road that leads to life and only a few find it" (Matthew 7:13-14, NIV).

God's Redemption of Darkness

"I will give you the treasures of darkness, riches stored in secret places, so that you may know that I am the Lord" (Isaiah 45:3, NIV). During one of the toughest places in my life, I found this comforting verse. I have shared it with countless people who have been experiencing a dark time in their own lives. The truth of this verse prevails over everything tragic we, as human beings, must face during our relatively short time here on earth. But, it is in the very midst of our biggest trials that God shows up with His mercy and grace to give us strength to carry on.

Hymn writer, Rev. Henry Lytes, penned the words to "Abide With Me" just one month before he died of tuberculosis. The words are so powerful that this song was played at Queen Elizabeth's wedding and also at Mother Teresa's funeral. "Abide with me; fast falls the even tide, The darkness deepens, Lord with me abide. When other helpers fail and comforts flee, Help of the helpless, O abide with me."

Are you going through a really rough time in your life right now? No matter where you look, there seems to be no hope? Well, you are not alone, my friend, for our God is there with you in the midst of your darkest hour if you belong to Him. Only His light will show you the way out of the dark.

God made a way for Patricia Riley Jones on May 21, 1990, when she found her beloved mother Ella Foy Riley savagely murdered. Words could never explain the dark horror and despair she faced at that moment. "Vengeance is mine," He spoke in her heart. "I will repay." Somehow, she and her entire family made it through the darkness. Pat's subsequent work with "Victims of Crime and Leniency" provided hope and help for others, who, like her family, experienced their own tragedies of personal loss at the hands of another murderer. God took her pain and turned it into a purpose for good, not evil.

Having a loved one diagnosed with Alzheimer's is a devastating experience. Looking after someone you love while their own remembrance of you fades slowly away, proves to be a plunge into a continuing nightmare. Today, Kay Jones, helps others as head of the area Alzheimer's Foundation. She can understand their hurts, because she lived with her own mother's battle with this dread disease.

"God can make a way for you, when there seems to be no way" are the words to a popular Christian tune now being heard on radio. If you'll only let Him, He can bring good out of your darkest hours and give you His richest treasures. He proved that He could for me.

What Does Resurrection Really Mean?

The simple meaning of "resurrection" in Webster's dictionary is "to raise from the dead." Of course, the resurrection of Jesus Christ is miraculous. There can be some other meaningful analogies, however, that will still affect human behavior in regards to a resurrection experience.

When our grandson, Nicholas, was only three, he was riding home with us from church one Easter Sunday when I asked him what the real meaning of Easter was. Quickly, he responded with, "Jesus 'wose' from the dead." I was thrilled that he knew the correct answer until seconds later when he quietly asked, "Nana, what does 'wose' from the dead mean?" Well, my husband and I tried to stifle our giggles as I attempted to explain this to him.

Unfortunately, even a number of adults don't understand what a "resurrection" or a "rising from the dead" actually means. In the example of Jesus's resurrection, it opened the way for true believers to achieve eternal life with Him. But, I believe what Jesus did for us can be an example of other types of "rising from the dead."

All of us have our own dreams and hopes for our future. What happens when that dream has to die? Take for example, the young teacher named Krista who desired to have a baby. The medication her husband had to take caused him to be sterile. Because she was a Christian, according to her belief, she had no other alternative to having a child of her own, so she had to die to her dream of having children. But...God! He is the author of the resurrection of dead dreams. Today in church,

Krista's Dad announced that she is expecting a baby. Remember that God, not man, has the final answer.

Then, there's the case of the high school drop-out who couldn't pass the tenth grade. Years later, after discovering he had a learning disability, he was able to graduate with honors from medical school and became a highly decorated surgeon general in the army. One spectacular night, his hometown high school gave him his coveted high school diploma in a special ceremony in his honor. "That was the one thing I never thought I'd ever receive," he was quoted as saying. He enjoyed immensely the resurrection of his dead dream.

Do you have a hope or a dream that has died? If it is in God's will for your life, it is always possible to see that desire "rise from the dead" and be fulfilled. That's the kind of God He is.

- "I want to know Christ and the power of his resurrection" (Philippians 3:10-11, NIV)
- "Jesus said to her, 'I am the resurrection and the life. He who believes in me will live, even though he dies" (John 11:25, NIV).

When you Desire a Great Blessing

In the fall of 1959, while I was a student at Huntingdon College in Montgomery, Alabama, I participated in something that could have seriously damaged my life. A group of my friends had gathered in my room to allow a fellow student (who had just returned from Spain) to read her Tarot cards in order to reveal to us our future. Even then, as a young Christian, I sensed that it was wrong, but I didn't have the courage to speak up against it. One by one, the "reader" of the cards told each girl present what their future would hold. Even more astounding was the accuracy of her "predictions." In one instance, just as she had informed one girl that a male member of her family was even then going through a life-threatening emergency, (but he would live, she said), the phone rang with news that her beloved grandfather had just had a heart attack. As per the Tarot cards' interpretation, the elderly gentleman came through it just fine.

I'll never forget how I felt when the dark-haired young woman announced to me that I would get married before I graduated from college. She further remarked that even though I would have numerous pets, I would never be able to have any children. I was heartbroken just hearing what she had predicted. It was impossible not to worry about it.

Soon after in my Biology lab, I discovered that I had A-negative blood. My professor explained that I could possibly suffer complications during pregnancy or even cause damage to my children if I had any. That only added to my feelings of doom.

Ironically, even though I had planned not to, I did marry before I graduated from Huntingdon. My wedding present from my husband was a Chihuahua puppy. Can't you just imagine how my fear was mounting as I remembered the "prediction" from the Tarot cards?

I did my graduate work at Auburn University after finishing my BA at Huntingdon and then began teaching school. By this time, I was beginning to really want a baby. In the back of my mind, however, no matter how hard I tried to push it out, was the fear that I would never be able to have a child.

My heart's desire was not only to be able to have a baby but to have a son. Since I had come from a family of four girls, I knew my own father would be so thrilled to have a grandson. During my prayer time, I began to ask God to show me how to pray and to believe Him for the answers.

Five long years passed, and I had still been unable to conceive. After the OB-gyn examined me, he told me that I had a very small pelvis, and that I might not be able to deliver a baby in the usual way. Therefore, if I did get pregnant, I would have to have a C-section most likely. That was another blow to digest.

Soon, all of our friends were either pregnant or giving birth to a baby. I was beginning to feel more and more desperate. My prayers intensified. They ranged from "Why" Why? Why?" to "I'll do anything you want me to do, Lord, just please let me get pregnant." One morning, I got up as usual and before reading my devotional for the day, I fell on my knees beside my bed. To the best of my remembrance, this was the prayer I prayed: "Lord, please forgive me for listening to those Tarot cards being read. I refuse to believe what was spoken is the truth, and I'm ashamed I ever participated in this sinful practice." Then I begged, "Lord, if you'll forgive me and open my womb so I can conceive, I'll give you back my son all the days of his life."

Just as soon as I had completed my prayer, I felt at total peace. It was if I had managed to "break through to God" and I sensed my answer was on its way. After pouring my cup full of coffee, I settled into my easy chair and picked up my devotional book. The passage was a familiar one, and now, one of the most precious in my life. It was 1 Samuel 1:9-18. Verse eleven literally leaped off the page at me. "O Lord of hosts, if thou wilt indeed look on the affliction of thine handmaid, and remember me....but wilt give unto thine handmaid a man child, then I will give him unto the Lord all the days of his life" (1 Samuel 1:9-18, KJV). If I had read that passage first, and then prayed, it wouldn't have been so significant, but I had prayed in faith before I knew what my devotional reading was for the day. From that morning on, I believed God was going to allow me to have a son.

That happened in December and in January, we went to the Orange Bowl in Miami to watch our Auburn Tigers get beaten by the Arkansas Razorbacks. During half-time when I went to the bathroom, I discovered that I was not pregnant. "But, I will be!" I announced to myself out loud. The very next month right after Valentine's Day, in fact, I went to see the Ob-Gyn, Dr. Clyde Smith. As he came in the door he asked me why I was there. "I want you to tell me I'm pregnant and I'm going to have a son" I said. Grinning, Dr. Smith said, "O. K. you are and you will, (Without even examining me). Of course, he eventually did the examination and true to his word, I was pregnant.

For all the nine months that I carried my baby, I prayed over my child and believed he was given to me by God. I didn't worry about my negative blood or my too narrow pelvis. Since this was before the days of ultra-sounds, I didn't know whether my baby was male or female. Even though I wanted a son very much, I promised the Lord that either way, I would be happy. Many, many times I kept reminding the Lord, that this child belonged to Him.

On November 11, 1964, Nurse Gwen McAllister laid the most beautiful baby boy in my arms just as I was waking up from his delivery. She chuckled, "Well, you got your wish, you have a son, and he's got a head full of hair!" I looked into my tiny baby's dark eyes and spoke these words, "God gave you to me, but you really belong to him."

That night I felt the presence of someone very dear to me in that hospital room. At first, I thought it might be my dear grandmother, Mama Annie, who had died many years before then, but almost immediately, I remembered that the dead can't return to visit the living. Then, I was made aware that what I sensed was the very presence of my Lord. "Father, my son, Trant, belongs to you. Do in his life what you choose to do" I prayed.

The waiting had been long, but God's mercy is always faithful. He does care about our deepest desires. In fact, I believe when we trust Him, He puts the right desires in our heart. That's exactly what I've been sharing with women who, like me, desire to have a baby when the wait seems impossibly long. God has even given me, on many occasions, the faith to believe for another person to get pregnant. There are numerous "prayer" babies now in my life, including, most recently, the birth of a baby girl to my niece Shannan after years of trying. This baby is our little Lucy. God can always move more readily when it is impossible!

The Greatest Gift of All is Love

Today is Valentine's Day when loved ones are remembered with a special token of their love. That is as it should be, but the gift is not as important as the true emotion behind what is given. The Bible gives us a beautiful description of real love. "Love is patient, love is kind. It does not envy, it does not boast, it is not proud. It is not rude, it is not self-seeking, it is not easily angered, it keeps no record of wrongs...It always protects, always trusts, always hopes, always perseveres. Love never fails" (1 Corinthians 13:4-8, NIV).

If that kind of love were truly put into practice, there would be no more divorces and probably no more problem children. The only way one can possess this love is to first of all know the love that can be found only in receiving the gift of salvation from the Lover of our souls, the Lord Jesus Christ.

The following story is an example of true godly love. On their wedding day, a young couple set out for their honeymoon. The bride, in her beautiful wedding gown, had to be tucked carefully into the tiny little volkswagon that was to be their transportation. A very short time later, a drunk driver ran a red light and plowed into the side of the small car where the bride was sitting. Tragically, she was left paralyzed from the shoulders down. That groom could have easily chosen to leave her then. After all, they had only been wed a short time before the accident. He didn't do that, however, but instead, spent the rest of his life loving and caring for that woman he pledged his life to. I interviewed them after they had raised two wonderful children, a son and a daughter. Even though their mother had never been able to properly hold the children as they grew up, they both had the security of knowing how much their parents genuinely loved and cared for each other, and their lives were tremendously enriched by that fact.

A very great man confided once that as a young boy all he ever prayed for every night was that his parents would love each other. It is true that the greatest gift parents may give a child is to love each other. The way you treat your spouse speaks volumes as to your faith and your commitment to Christ.

In Genesis, we read how much Jacob loved Rachel. Even though he worked for seven years to buy her from her father, Laban, it is recorded that "the years seemed like only a few days to him because of his love for her" (Genesis 29:18, NIV).

In an age where couples choose to divorce for the most insignificant reasons, they don't seem to realize the tragic fall out it causes with their children. That is why I am so thankful for my husband, Jerome, who has committed his love to me for all these years. When I look at him, I don't see his receding hairline, the wrinkles on his face or even the little tummy he is now getting. Not really. That doesn't matter at all. What I do see is a man who loves the Lord with all of his heart and loves me like that as well. I hope he doesn't just see my aging face and body either but simply knows how much I truly love and respect him. He will be my valentine forever.

The Prayer That Changed a Life Forever

There might come a time in your life when you will have the opportunity to be the instrument that may radically change someone else's life. The following is a true story of how a public school teacher in New York State did just that. When the problem arose, the dedicated teacher wanted to do something desperately but she did not know what she could possibly do about the situation. As usual, she went to the Lord and prayed for His guidance. Krista's young student had seemed well adjusted when she first came into the classroom at the beginning of the year. Teacher and pupil quickly bonded. The young girl(I will call her Mary) was living with her father and step-mother that had fought for custody of her and had won after a long battle. All went well until summer vacation was approaching and everything started to fall apart.

One day Mary came to school unusually withdrawn and sad looking. Krista tried to carry on a conversation with her student but there was little response. Not knowing what the problem was, the young teacher decided to say nothing and wait to see if Mary would eventually confide in her. For a week or so, there was no opening for Krista to approach her little friend. Since she had been a pastor's daughter and knew the power of prayer for herself, she began to earnestly pray that God would show her the reason for the change in the student's countenance.

She realized that she was very limited as to how much she could get involved with her student's personal problems. The teacher could suggest that they speak to the school guidance counselor. Krista waited without a clear directive as to how she could help. Each day as she prayed for Mary, it became evident that something was so drastically wrong that something had to be done immediately. Her first thought was that her father or her step-mother might be hurting this child. Both of them seemed very kind and concerned about Mary's progress and didn't appear to be the type to be abusive parents.

Then, Krista saw the tell-tale marks on her student's arms and legs. There was no doubt. Mary was cutting herself. The revelation of this fact hurt Krista deeply because she knew of other children (girls mostly) who would deliberately hurt themselves. After studying these cases, Krista knew that the incidents would not stop without serious intervention and only if the facts became know as to what was causing this bizarre behavior. Worse than anything was the escalation of this torment. Once it started, it would continue and grow even more brutal and with greater frequency.

After Krista learned that her pupil had been cutting herself, she watched as this formerly cheerful child grew more and more despondent. The compassionate teacher prayed that she could find a way to help Mary. Then one day, the girl came rushing into class asking to talk to her teacher. Thankfully, it was on a day that there was an aide in the classroom and Krista could turn her lessons over to the intern while she had time to talk to Mary.

That was the first answered prayer that the little girl had come to her asking her to help. What the young woman heard both shocked and angered her. Krista could hardly believe what she was hearing. In tears, Mary poured out her fears concerning her biological mother. It was more than just the continuous threat of beatings and other cruelty that her mother had heaped on her. Before Mary had moved to New York to live with her father, her mother had promised to kill her one day and bury her body somewhere that no one would ever be able to find her. It was evident that the cuttings had begun as a coping mechanism. Mary could focus on the physical pain and so distract herself from dealing with the emotional pain and fear. The counselor her father had sent her to had taken all her click pens and spiral bound notebooks away from her because the metal springs was what she was using to hurt herself.

The State of New York had ordered Mary to go visit her mother in the summer months and now it was almost time to go. The child was terrified. That was the day the brave teacher took the little girl into her arms and with the child's permission, prayed for her. Krista asked God to somehow intervene and protect her from the threats of her mother. She prayed in faith not knowing what would happen to her job if anyone found out that she had so boldly prayed in a public school. Krista could only pray over and over, "Lord, have mercy on this child. You are a God of Mercy. Please Father, demonstrate your love and your power to this child. Lord whatever you need to do, please do it quickly. The time is running out and we need a miracle"

What happened after that could only be explained as the intervention of a Loving God. At the next counseling session with her psychologist, Mary opened up and told him everything that she was afraid of just as her teacher had instructed her to do. "Don't be afraid; you've got to tell the whole truth." Amazingly, this secular but kindly psychologist must have experienced a divine impulse because he took matters into his own hands after hearing what his frightened client revealed to him. He not only picked up the phone and called Mary's mother, but he boldly informed her that her daughter was not coming for a visit that summer, or for that matter, he added, "She will never be coming there again!" His declaration was followed exactly. Krista's prayers had been answered in a miraculous way and now, Mary is back to her normal self and evidently very happy with her father and step-mother.

More things are accomplished by prayer than by all the weapons of this world. Ask God to give you the desire to help change the circumstances in someone's life. The answer is only a prayer away.

- "Is any one of you in trouble? He should pray" (James 5:13, NIV).
- "The prayer of a righteous man is powerful and effective" (James 5:16, NIV).
- "Therefore I tell you, whatever you ask for in prayer, believe that you have received it, and it will be yours" (Mark 11:25, NIV).

Honoring Your Parents is not an Option

Mother's Day is over, but Father's Day will be here soon. Celebrations of both those events are wonderful. However, just giving a gift, sending a card or making a phone call to Mom or Dad is not enough. What every parent wants is for their child to spend time with them and if that is not always possible, just expressing your thanks and love will mean everything to them. When my mother died, I found all the letters and even the framed little poems I had written to both my parents. I knew that they had treasured these words of love to them.

Only one commandment in the Bible carries with it the promise of a fulfilling and long life. "Children obey your parents in the Lord, for this is right. Honor your father and mother which is the first commandment with a promise that it may go well with you and that you may enjoy long life on the earth" (Eph 6:1-3, NIV).

We usually have to obey our parents when we are young and not every parent was a good one. Most of us, however, in spite of our mistakes did the best we could. I encourage every person who reads this to know that in spite of all your parents' imperfections, they all loved you very much. Do you still honor and respect them now that they are old and you are grown? Do you still want to visit them or in some way let them know how much you still value them? And, not just on Mother's or Father's Day but every day.

I will always remember one of the ways my son, Trant, made me feel so special. When he was nine years old, he made me a necklace our of gem clips. Each one was patiently covered with sticky shelving paper that was a bright hue of lime green with diagonal olive splashes. I wore that necklace everywhere even when the check-out girl at the grocery store stopped mid sentence as she was complimenting it when she suddenly observed a few of the gem clips peeking out of the paper. I explained that my dear son had lovingly crafted that necklace just for me because he loved me. It still brings tears to my eyes when I think about it.

There is also the Mother's Day card that my daughter Paige wrote to me about how much she now appreciated me even though she didn't always feel that way growing up. She apologized for not always being the best daughter to me and only prayed that one day her own children would honor and respect her just like she did me.

While on his recent honeymoon, Ben Braswell wrote a three page letter to his parents thanking them for all the ways they had worked to make his life so great. He added that he only hoped when he and his new bride, Holly, had children that they could do as good as his parents had done.

If you really want to experience a real high, I encourage you to let your parents know how much you love and appreciate them, if you are fortunate to still have your parents. Write them a love letter or even an e-mail. Choose to call them, visit them and show them how much you appreciate all they have done for you. After all, they spent a great deal of time bringing you up. Don't have regrets when they are no longer here.

Why you Have to Forgive

It may start with a simple feeling of irritation with another person. Next, it escalates to a belief that an individual is somehow taking advantage of you or using you. Soon, you begin to re-hash everything the offending person has ever done to you – real or just imagined. You tell someone and in speaking about the offense, your heart begins to beat faster. Your body feels flushed with heat. Because you have become so emotionally and, now, physically involved, the truth of the matter is that the person you feel has so "wronged" you now owns you!

No matter how deeply you have been hurt by someone, it will only bring you additional harm if you can't forgive. Ask yourself this question. Is there anyone whose presence or even the mention of their name causes your heart rate to increase? Is there anyone who can totally cause you to become angry, bitter and often behave irrationally?

If just thinking about someone causes you to get upset, then it is obvious that person has you under their power. In essence, they control you! The only way to achieve freedom is to "let it go." Ask God to help you to dig out all the bitterness in your heart against that person or anyone else who can affect the way you go about your daily life.

If you have a root of bitterness, it will ultimately hurt you far more than your unforgiveness will hurt that other individual.

There was a woman who had been divorced for over 40 years, but she talked about the wrong done to her every day. Ultimately, it cost her in more ways than one. She lost her health and the respect of her children.

A missionary's wife shared a simple recipe for helping a person practice the doctrine of forgiveness. Mrs. Stringer said,

"If you honestly want to forgive someone then first no longer "nurse" the wrong done to you. That means give it up and don't hold on to it as something dear to your heart. Secondly, don't "rehearse" it. In other words, quit talking to everyone else about how wronged you have been by that other person you are bitter against. Then, finally, "disperse" it." Meaning, of course, give it to God. You have to ask our Heavenly Father to take it from you. God would never command us to "forgive" if He wasn't willing to give us the power to do so. Our first responsibility is to be willing to forgive.

Another little formula that might get you on the right path to forgiveness was shared in a women's retreat years ago. It's called "Building a Brick House." First, lay the foundation to your house – be willing to forgive. The side of your "house" is refusing to discuss the wrong anymore with anyone. In fact, try to say something good about your "enemy" instead. The top is beginning to pray for the one who has wronged you. That means praying for God to bless them, not for lightning to strike them! At last, the other side of your imaginary brick house is asking God to show you something good that you could do for the person who has hurt you.

If you will honestly follow these simple suggestions, the person you have considered your bitter adversary will do one or two things. He or she will behave differently toward you, even sometimes by becoming your friend. Or, with your change in behavior, they'll stay as far away from you as possible and will cause you no more grief.

Remember, our best guide to destroying all bitterness and achieving true forgiveness if found in God's word.

- "See to it that no one misses the grace of God and that no bitter root forms up to cause trouble and defile many" (Hebrews 12:15, NIV).

- "Be kind and compassionate to one another, forgiving each other, just as in Christ, God forgave you" (Ephesians 4:32, NIV).

The Best Laid Plans Are not Always the Best

Have you ever wanted something so much that you were tempted to take matters into your own hands and "make it happen?" In the Bible, Sarah desired a child so desperately that she forgot what God had promised her. Urging her husband she said, "The Lord has kept me from having children. Go, sleep with my maidservant; perhaps I can build a family through her" (Genesis 16:2, NIV).

Well, you know what happened? Sarah helped create "Ishmael", and his descendants have been at war ever since with Sarah's true offspring. Her beloved son, Isaac was finally born according to God's promise.

Sarah designed this meticulous plan, but God was not in it. How many times have we been guilty of the same thing? All of us have probably created our own "Ishmaels" at some time or other.

Once, my husband and I felt that God wanted us to start a counseling ministry, so when doors didn't open like we thought they should, we set out to do something to cause those doors to open. That's when we came up with the plan to open a business to help fund the ministry. Unfortunately we lost a lot of money before our business failed. Even though our motive may have been right, we had rushed in without God's blessing.

Unfortunately, I know of more than one case where a woman had made up her mind to have a husband no matter what. Even if it meant going shopping for him, it didn't matter. Sadly, many times a marriage does occur, but it inevitably ends in divorce. Why? Because the intricate web woven to capture a husband had nothing to do with God's will. That's why it fell apart.

Even on our recent vacation, we thought all of our plans were set in stone. Were we ever misdirected! We had trusted in the wrong person, and when we arrived at our destination, there were no tickets available. We had to ask God to give us His plans for the week-end. Thankfully, He did.

Rule number one: Believe what God says in His word and according to His character. Never plan anything without His blessing and direction no matter how strongly you feel motivated.

Rule number two: Wait, if necessary on and on until He opens a door. Instead of your well-laid plans, trust Him to arrange His plans for your life. "Many are the plans in a man's heart, but it is the Lord's purpose that prevails" (Proverbs 19:21, NIV).

When is it Right to Lie?

Ever told a "little white lie?" Or, at least that's what we convince ourselves it is. Is lying always wrong? What about telling a little white lie to protect yourself? Like if you told the truth you could get in trouble? Your secrets might come out, so wouldn't it be better and easier to say something that is not exactly the whole truth?

The fact of the matter is we have become a society of people who are learning how to avoid leaving our comfort zones. Lying is now an accepted practice by many. It was not always this way.

Many years ago, a man was told that his daughter had knocked some sheets from a neighbor's clothes line causing them to be soiled. When the father questioned his child, she vehemently denied it. Since, in his mind, lying was far worse than this deed, he urged her to tell the truth. When she insisted on her innocence, he gave her a severe whipping. Tragically, the girl died as a result. Ironically, her Daddy was never punished for what he did as he obviously hadn't meant to kill his daughter.

Another twist to the story happened at the funeral when the neighbor came in and told the family that her own two children had confessed to damaging the sheets. Their daughter had been falsely accused. According to the man's granddaughter (who told me this story), he never got over what he had done even though his actions had been the result of believing lying was a vile sin.

How do you answer when someone asks you if they look fat, or if you like their new hairstyle? Are you always truthful, or is it easier to lie rather than risk being disliked?

All lying is serious. It is never right to lie and according to God's standards, there is no such thing as a "little white lie." Granted, we all struggle with this temptation to lie. Often times, telling the truth is quite costly, but then, on the other hand, lying and its consequence is far more dangerous. My father believed if a man would lie, he would also steal.

The truth is preferred since "A man of perverse heart does not prosper, he whose tongue is deceitful falls into trouble" (Proverbs 17:20, NIV). Therefore, "Keep your tongue from evil and your lips from speaking lies" (Psalm 34:13, NIV).

So, the next time a situation arises when you have to choose between lying and telling the truth, always tell the truth. Remember that the Lord knows your heart for "Before a word is on my tongue you know it completely, O Lord" (Psalm 139:4, NIV).

Rainbow People in the Midst of Clouds

Clouds come and darken our horizon. Days are sometimes dark and dreary for us all. Even in the midst of the storms of our lives, God has promised a blessing for those whose trust is unwaveringly in Him. God made a promise to His children by way of covenant. "I have set my rainbow in the clouds, and it will be the sign of the covenant between me and the earth" (Genesis 9:13, NIV). The difficult circumstances come, but we can survive when we know His rainbow of hope is waiting. When those dark times come, God can raise up someone who can offer the gift of encouragement and bring peace even in the midst of our most trying circumstances. I choose to be that kind of person.

For guidance, Edward E. Hale has said, "Look up and not down; look forward and not back; look out and not in; lend a hand." I believe that it is for our own benefit when we are suffering in some way for us to look to the needs of others. Even a shut-in can pray for God to bless someone else. There are many who are always up and about their "Father's business" as Jesus was. Others, however, choose to wallow in self-pity and cry out, "why me" when troubles come. "Know that the Lord has set apart the godly for himself; the Lord will hear when I call to him" (Psalm 4:3, NIV).

Her name was "Miss Susie" and she was a true servant of the Lord. When the women of our church had a luncheon, it was this tiny silver-haired lady that waited on the tables and then loaded up the dishes and washed them. She always had a glowing smile on her face. One day I walked out in time to see her catch a cab. I learned later that her husband was an invalid, and they lived in a tiny apartment. They didn't even have a car of their own, but it didn't stop this lady from being a minister to others. I want to be like "Miss Susie."

Harvey was a janitor at WTVY, but he was much more than that. This man had found Jesus, and he went above and beyond to make our life better. At daybreak, he was at work making coffee for the early morning staff even though his shift did not begin until hours after then. Smiles always wreathed his face even when he was in pain. None of us knew, not even Harvey, that he had terminal cancer. One day, when he didn't come to work, we all knew something was wrong. Harvey had gone to be with Jesus in his sleep. WTVY turned out at his funeral to honor our co-worker and friend.

Choose today how you want to live out this coming year. You can be a blessing or you can be a grouch. Rainbows are beautiful and fill us with hope. I am praying that I will always be a messenger of encouragement in this world filled with trials.

The Grass Always Looks Greener on the Other Side

Riding out in the country a few weeks ago, I saw a big tan and white cow straining her head through a barbed wire fence in an attempt to munch a tuff of green grass. Pointing this out to my husband, I commented that the cow had plenty of good grass all around where she was standing but what she was reaching for was actually a butterweed.

This does illustrate a point, however, for just like the misguided cow, we humans always think that other people have it better than we do. When we see the appearance that people are prone to project, we may conclude that this marriage or family is perfect, when, in truth, that projected façade is just that – a show, and not a reality.

For example, years ago a dear friend of mine confided that early in her marriage she had observed another couple who looked "so happy." She secretly wished that her husband would act just like this man. He was so attentive to his wife and appeared to be very romantic, whereas, her own husband never seemed to pay any attention to her. Was she surprised to discover that the couple she so admired eventually wound up divorced due to the husband's infidelity.

Many a man (or woman) has strayed from their marriage covenant only to discover what dazzled them was all fake. I remember talking to a very prominent man in another city who told me that he had left his wife and children for this "beautiful woman" who eventually ran off and deserted him for another man. The saddest part of all was the very real possibility that my acquaintance would grow old alone. He confessed that he almost choked up every time he saw an elderly couple strolling along the beach together – arm in arm.

In the Bible, the "lure" of other things has cost one biblical character his health. Gehazi, servant of Elisha, desired the rewards offered by Naaman from Aram who had been healed by God's intervention. After receiving the ill-gotten gains, he also got Naaman's leprosy. (See 2 Kings 5:9-27).

We all remember Eve (and Adam, too) who reached for the one thing God had forbidden in the Garden of Eden. This rebellious act plunged the world from then on into sin. "When the woman saw that the fruit of the tree was good for food and pleasing to the eye, and also desirable for gaining wisdom, she took some and ate it. She also gave some to her husband, who was with her, and he ate it" (Genesis 3:6).

King David was a man after God's own heart but he lusted after another man's wife. Bathsheba was the only wife of David's trusted soldier, Uriah, the Hittite, and yet, in spite of all the wives and concubines David had, he also wanted this one woman. The consequences from this sin almost destroyed King David, and it did severely damage his entire family. (See I2 Samuel 11:1-5).

If we believe what God's word says, we can resist temptation. We don't have to be looking elsewhere for satisfaction. The enemy of our souls, Satan, wants us to fail and to fall. That's why the "whatever it is" looks so appealing from our viewpoint. It may be a forbidden fruit, an improper relationship or a greedy longing for wealth. Satan knows our weakest areas, and he'll do everything he can to snare each person.

We can choose to be satisfied always like the apostle Paul, who said, "for I have learned to be content whatever the circumstances" (Philippians 4:11b, NIV).

In Hebrews 13:5 the Godly advice is "be content with what you have, because God has said, never will I leave you, never will I forsake you." It is always wise to stay on our designated side of the fence. The fence that God has placed in our lives just like the farmer had built to protect his cows. God's fence is our protection.

God's Scheduled Appointments

"In his heart a man plans his course, but the Lord determines his steps" (Proverbs 16:9, NIV).

A few weeks ago on a flight to Hartford, Connecticut, my husband and I saw some moments of God's intervention in many everyday events of our lives. Before leaving, we had prayed together asking God to use us in all the lives of those we saw during our trip. The first encounter occurred when a young career woman "just happened" to have been given a seat next to mine on the plane. It was not long before we were chatting like old friends and after only a short span of time, she was confiding in me concerning some of her present struggles in the business world, as well as in her personal life.

Looking back, I realize that it was certainly not by accident that we were seatmates. Her mother had recently died and ironically, this lady was originally from Montgomery, Alabama. I shared with her that I had done my undergraduate work at Huntingdon College there in her home town and my graduate work at Auburn University. Gail (not her real name) smiled as she told me that she, too, had completed school at Auburn with a degree in Mechanical Engineering. Presently, she was flying back to Hartford after attending a business conference in Orlando.

The more we talked, the more I was aware of her deep hurt and I did my best to share with her how it was possible to roll her problems over on God. As I became bolder in my statements concerning faith, she suddenly began to cry. It was all I could do, as a mother myself, not to just wrap my arms around her and promise her that everything would be all right. Her mother had been her confidant and she missed her terribly. I gave her some Scriptures to study, promised to pray about her two situations (job and personal issues) and by the time we landed I think we had experienced a tremendous breakthrough for her. I emailed her last night and plan to keep up with her. One thing I did tell her was I believed that God had arranged for us to sit together that day just like He had made it possible for another lady years ago to sit by me on a flight to New Orleans to visit my doctor when I was struggling to overcome lupus. All those years ago, another motherly woman had given me great hope during one of the darkest periods of my life. "It's not always going to be like this," she had said. You are going to have a whole new life ahead of you." The minute I told "Gail" this story, she teared up again. Inwardly, I was reminded again that what the older woman had told me years ago had truly come to pass. We serve an awesome God.

After we landed, "Gail" walked us down to get our luggage, we hugged and she turned to leave as her ride had come to pick her up. I waved "good-bye" and we went to our bus that was to take us to the place where we had our rental car ready. Even though we were very tired from traveling, Jerome and I were very encouraged just knowing that along the way, we had helped to share the burdens of another person.

Just look around you, God will use you if you will just let him. It may be a person at your grocery store, a clerk in the department store, your mailman or guy that services your car, but there are so many hurting people around us that need some hope. As a dear country lady once said, "Lord, I just pray that you will please 'hope' me a minute." I'm sure it was just the way she spoke "help" but it rang true enough to me the way I heard it. Are you willing to "hope" someone put in your path today? If so, don't be surprised at where God places you next.

When Snow Ushered in a Miracle on Christmas Eve

"My thoughts are completely different from yours," says the LORD. "And my ways are far beyond anything you could imagine" (Isaiah 55:8, NIV).

The year was 1989. Mike and Laura Everett had just welcomed their first child into the world. Little Ryland had been born on December 11th. Sadly, however, after 3 separate tests were run, the 72 hour one had indicated he had contracted group B strep infection. Little Ryland had to have IVs in his head, arm and leg because the sites deteriorated rapidly in an infant.

The couple had looked so forward to having their son home for Christmas, but it looked impossible. All of their friends and family had earnestly prayed, but the tiny baby was not getting any better.

On Christmas eve, Mike arrived at the hospital to visit with his son and his wife, Laura. Because he had not eaten anything for awhile, Mike decided to run down to the hospital cafeteria to get something to eat. As he bowed his head to pray for God's blessing on his food, and also, for God to somehow intervene in his young child's life, something quickened in his spirit.

As he finished his prayer, he turned to watch as others in the cafeteria were rushing to the windows to look outside. It was snowing on Christmas Eve in South Alabama!!! Everett was suddenly filled with joy. Somehow, the snow seemed like a sign of some kind. It was certainly way out of the ordinary. For the first time since he discovered Ryland's illness, Mike felt the real

Christmas spirit; moreover he knew in his heart his son would get well.

When he rushed up in the elevator to go check on his wife and son, he found Laura sitting beside little Ryland's bed. There had been no word yet that day about his present condition. After telling his wife about the falling snow, the couple, together, watched as the beautiful white mist fell, blanketing all the grass and trees. They looked at each other and grinned "Can you believe it? This never happens in Dothan, Alabama" Mike exclaimed. "It's a miracle!"

Just then, a door opened and they turned to look at the attending physician as he walked into the room. He bent down over little Ryland's bed to place his stethoscope on the tiny chest. After examining the infant thoroughly, he straightened up, took a deep breath and said, "This is rather amazing, Mr. and Mrs. Everett, your baby is almost completely well. You can take him home now if you want to." The Everetts were overjoyed as they began bundling up their newborn to get him released from the hospital.

And that's how little Ryland was able to spend his first Christmas at home with his mom and dad. All the while, the beautiful snow was lazily building up outside.

God's ways may catch us by surprise, but they are always designed for our best.

Why I Believe There is a Heaven

Once a self-described atheist stood at the caskets of both his godly parents who had recently been killed at the very same time in a freak automobile accident. As he stared intently into first one and then the other face of his beloved parents, a great sense of peace engulfed him. Looking at all the goodness in those two faces, he became suddenly aware that their lives could not possibly be over. It was far stronger than just "wishful thinking." It was as if God had moved in and taken away his "stony heart" and just as quickly replaced it with a "heart of flesh." "I will give you a new heart and put a new spirit in you; I will remove from you your heart of stone and give you a heart of flesh" (Ezekiel 36:26, NIV).

The man walked out of the funeral home a new person. It took the tragic death of his parents to cause his spiritually blind eyes to be opened. He finally realized the joy of salvation and the promise of life after death in Heaven. Ironically, after years of praying and believing for the salvation of their son, at last those prayers were answered.

On a Sunday morning during his Sunday School Class, Russ Ragan answered his teacher's question about why he was glad he became a Christian. "Because I know where I'll spend eternity," he confidently replied. Shortly after this time, Russ's plane nose dived into a dry lake bed, and he was instantly killed. But, Russell Ragan is not dead, for the word of God promises "Absent from the body and present with the Lord" (2 Corinthians 5:6, NIV). Ragan believed this, and today he is forever with his Lord.

My granddaughter Cassidy, age 8, assured her friend Elizabeth that if she asked Jesus to come into her heart she could go to Heaven forever and see all her pets that had died before. She also added, "But if you don't get saved, you'll go to Hell, and it's a really bad place with no cats and dogs." Her theology might not be 100%, but she certainly is on the right track.

Countless thousands have been martyred for their faith in Christ. How could they have endured without believing in the promise of their Heavenly Home? I do not doubt there is a Heaven to gain and a place called Hell to escape from. There is overwhelming evidence in the Bible that Heaven is a reality. There are so many verses I could give you, but here are a few of my favorite.

- "Rejoice and be glad, because great is your reward in Heaven" (Matthew 5:12, NIV).
- "In my Father's house are many rooms; if it were not so, I would have told you. I am going there to prepare a place for you" (John 14:2-3, NIV).
- "But store up for yourselves treasures in heaven, where moth and rust do not destroy, and where thieves do not break in and steal" (Matthew 6:20, NIV).
- "When the dead rise, they will neither marry nor be given in marriage; they will be like the angels in heaven" (Mark 12:25, NIV).
- "Men of Galilee," they said, "why do you stand here looking into the sky? This same Jesus, who has been taken from you into heaven, will come back in the same way you have seen him go into heaven" (Acts 1:11, NIV).
- 'To the church of the firstborn, whose names are written in heaven. You have come to God, the judge of all men, to the spirits of righteous men made perfect" (Hebrews 12:23, NIV).
- "And I heard a loud voice from the throne saying, "now the dwelling of God is with men, and he will live with

them. They will be his people, and God himself will be with them and be their God" (Revelation 21:3, NIV).

I believe in Heaven, do you?

A Simple Act of Kindness Can Show God's Love

Love is more than a feeling, it is an act of our will to show love to others. Kindness is a genuine way of showing that each person is of great value just like God reveals in the Scriptures. Jesus even commanded those who followed him to have this type of love : "A new command I give you: Love one another. As I have loved you, so you must love one another" (John 13:34, NIV). How often Christians will argue that this means to love only those we are close to in the body of Christ, but then Jesus also said, "love your neighbor as yourself" (Matthew 19:19, NIV).

We are human and often find it very difficult to even love those in the Christian faith. How much more challenging it is then to actually show our love to others who might not even be believers? Yet, love is the force that can change lives.

A few weeks back, a story broke in all the news media and was seen even on "you tube" about an unusual high school football game played in Grapevine, Texas. Faith Academy (a Christian private school) was scheduled to host a game with the Gainesville State School (a high-security youth correctional facility). The coach of Faith Academy was inspired to do a marvelous deed to show those convicted youth a lesson in love. He asked half of the parents of his students and half of the cheerleaders to support the other team. Even though it was very difficult, they agreed. The results were amazing. Even though the Christian school won the game, the incarcerated youth in their old tattered equipment were moved to tears. Some said that no one had ever cheered for them before and certainly no one had ever called their names out to show support. At the end of the game, a group prayer was held and before the visiting team got on the bus, each received a hamburger, fries, a coke and a Bible. Hopefully, by showing the State school team the unconditional love and kindness that they did will make a difference in their lives. These young men were shown that they were valuable to God just as much as any other person on this planet.

Sheila Merritt wrote to tell me how she and her husband had honored a great aunt and uncle who had been unable to attend their wedding due to their age and health. The bride and groom then decided to do something absolutely loving by driving all the way to Colquitt, Georgia still in their wedding attire to see the elderly couple. They even carried them refreshments from the reception. With faces lit up with pure joy, the aunt and uncle thanked the young couple who had delayed their honeymoon in order to honor these two people who had loved them so much.

Today, I challenge all of you to be aware of how you can show the love of Christ to people who might not have anyone else to do a kind deed for them. Believe me, try it and it is contagious. At our church, Calvary Baptist, we get little cards to use when we are going through a fast food restaurant and pay for the food ordered by the person in line behind us. No one knows who we are, but the card only says that we want to show them in a small measure how much God loves them. Remember, there is no power on earth greater than His love.

God Brings us out so He Can Bring us In

When the door bangs shut, our hearts grope with fear. What next for me, Lord? All of my confidence and hope have been placed in this one direction. All the things I have been familiar with, the pattern of happy days now gone forever. I can't go back. Yet, I don't have the will to go forward. Help me, Father, for my entire life is now on hold.

If this has been your heart cry in the past or maybe, just maybe, it is your present state of mind, look up, God is still watching out for you. When the children of Israel were miraculously delivered from slavery in Egypt, they still longed for the days that they had been accustomed to. How easily they had forgotten what they had been made to endure. "For the Lord has told you, 'You are not to go back that way again'" (Deuteronomy 17: 16, NIV). When He brings you out of something, it is because He intends to bring you in to something far better.

God is the same God that He has always been. He will act on our behalf to fulfill those plans He has made for our lives. "The lord said to Abram, after Lot had parted from him, 'Lift up your eyes from where you are, and look north and south, east and west for all the land that you see, I will give it to you and to your offspring forever'" (Genesis 13:14,15, NIV). Whatever has been "Lot" in your life has to be removed before God's blessings can fall on you and those you love.

The young woman lay on the couch for days in a hopeless state. A man she had trained had been promoted over her with twice the salary. Then one day, her mother said to her. "Get up, it's time to stop feeling sorry for yourself. You can do anything you set your mind to do." With only a dream and $5,000 in savings, this distraught woman got up and did something about her life. Mary Kay Ash founded Mary Kay Cosmetics. Not only did she provide for her own family, but she opened a door so that many, many other ladies could take care of their children and still be "stay at home moms" by selling this great line of cosmetics. Mary Kay put her faith first, her family second and her business third. When she died in 2001, her company was worth millions. If Mary Kay had gotten that promotion, she would have never started her successful business venture.

A few weeks ago, my husband, Jerome, experienced something wonderful. One morning while he was out walking, he suddenly remembered that right after we had bought the farm, he had found a beautiful white arrowhead out in the pasture. As he turned around to head back home, he prayed: "God, just how involved are you with our lives right now?" For some reason, he decided to walk back in the field that had been freshly plowed, and he felt led to walk down the third row of the mounded dirt. As he moved forward, he looked down and at his feet he found another perfect white arrowhead. It had probably been there for hundreds of years, and it had been a good 20 years since he had discovered the first one in the opposite pasture. The same Lord who showed him the first arrowhead was the same God who revealed the second one to him. What an amazing and true blessing. God will always be there for you. It doesn't matter where you are in life "the righteous will thrive like a green leaf" (Proverbs 11:28, NIV).

About the Author

Ann Varnum has hosted WTVY's talk shows since 1974 and presently does early morning news features, The Ann Varnum show on Saturday and Sunday Morning with Ann Varnum each Sunday. She writes a devotional column for The Dothan Eagle, the column "From the Heart of Dothan" for the Dothan Magazine, is a featured writer for the Wiregrass Living Magazine and does "Digging for Treasure" each week day on 91.7 American Family Radio.

Ann is married to Jerome Varnum and the couple has three married children and five grandchildren. They are members of Calvary Baptist Church in Dothan where Ann teaches an Intercessory Prayer Class on Wednesday nights.

Ann is a graduate of Huntingdon College in Montgomery, Alabama and did her graduate work at Auburn University. She is a free-lance writer who has been published often nationally and enjoys inspirational speaking. She has Co-Authored two cookbooks (with her sister Martha Lavallet) the Field O' Dreams Farm Cookbook Volume I and II. Ann has written her television memoirs "Sunny Side Up, An Inside Look at Early Morning TV."

Made in the USA
Charleston, SC
03 June 2011